THE UNFETTERED WORD

Southern Baptists Confront the Authority-Inerrancy Question

THE UNFETTERED WORD

Southern Baptists
Confront the
Authority-Inerrancy
Question

ROBISON B. JAMES
Editor

WORD BOOKS
PUBLISHER
WACO, TEXAS

A DIVISION OF
WORD, INCORPORATED

THE UNFETTERED WORD

Grateful acknowledgment is made for permission to reprint a revised version of "The Bible as Spiritual Friend" by Charles H. Talbert, which first appeared in the Spring 1986 issue of *Perspectives in Religious Studies*. It appears as chapter 3 in this volume. Permission is also gratefully acknowledged for the use of chapters 2–7, 9, and 11 which were originally published in *SBC Today* in 1986, 1987.

Library of Congress Cataloging-in-Publication Data

The Unfettered word : Southern Baptists confront the authority-
   inerrancy question / Robison B. James, editor.
      p.   cm.
   Bibliography: p.
   ISBN 0-8499-3094-4 :
   1. Bible—Evidences, authority, etc.   2. Bible—Inspiration.
   3. Southern Baptist Convention—Doctrines.   4. Baptists—Doctrines.
   I. James, Robison B., 1931–
BS480.U54 1987
220.1'3'088261—dc 19   87-20725
                                                              CIP

Printed in the United States of America
7898   BKC   987654321

Contents

Foreword

MARK A. NOLL

I was privileged to be one of the outside speakers at the Southern Baptist Conference on Biblical Inerrancy at Ridgecrest, North Carolina, in May 1987. The experience was eye opening for someone with very little firsthand contact with Southern Baptists. To the extent that the conference was representative, Southern Baptists are a people of great energy, fervent Christian devotion, and considerable rhetorical skill. They are also not entirely free of a genius for controversy.

The issue at the Ridgecrest meeting was itself of great importance. How would Southern Baptists think about Scripture? How would they maintain traditional Baptist faithfulness to the written Word of God? How would they work through current debates over the "inerrancy" of Scripture?

The Ridgecrest conference, with its combination of lectures by "Yankee evangelicals" and learned responses from Southern Baptists, did not end debate over the nature and authority of the Bible. But it did show how serious Southern Baptist leaders are about the question, and how hard many in that denomination are willing to work on the issue.

The questions discussed at Ridgecrest are also the central issues of this book. They are questions of great moment for the Southern Baptist Convention, the largest Protestant denomination in America, at the current stage in its development. Southern Baptists are moving out rapidly from their historic enclaves, both geographical and intellectual. They are moving toward a fuller involvement with the religious and intellectual life of the United States and the world at large. With this expansion has come new influence and prestige, but also fresh impetus to reexamine traditional beliefs and practices. The challenge is felt especially for the historic Southern Baptist confidence in the Bible.

Southern Baptists now confront the same sort of issues with which Presbyterians, Episcopalians, Methodists, and northern Baptists have been wrestling for at least a century. Put most simply, the question is how to remain faithful to the traditional Christian belief in an authoritative Scripture while participating in a world where leading centers of learning, a great deal of conventional wisdom, and even many church leaders dismiss the idea that the Bible is a unique revelation from God.

Recent controversy among Southern Baptists has focused on the tensions of that question. A tiny minority on the liberal fringe has seemed to agree that traditional convictions about the Bible need to be revamped entirely. A somewhat larger group at the other extreme seems unwilling to accept any modern insight about the Bible from any corner of the world whatsoever. Most Southern Baptists, however, fall between these extremes, and for them the debate can be intense.

One very important question in that debate concerns the use of the term *inerrancy* to describe the Bible. This question is the subject of *The Unfettered Word.* Its authors, with perhaps a few exceptions, do not feel that "inerrant" is the best word, or the most helpful word, to describe the character of the Bible. Most of the authors would call themselves "moderate conservatives" who fear damage to their church if the "fundamentalist conservatives" get their way and impose a strict view of inerrancy on the denomination.

The book is a thought-provoking one. Its chapters bring important considerations to the wider attention of Southern Baptists. It should be a helpful book that focuses Southern Baptist discussion on this crucial matter and opens up thinking among Southern Baptists to other Christians.

I am able to commend it even though, like many other sympathetic readers, I may disagree with some of its assertions. For example, I find that as a theologically conservative Presbyterian, I can affirm both a qualified doctrine of inerrancy and a relative openness to some forms of biblical criticism. I also happen to appreciate very much the work of the theologians from Princeton Seminary in the nineteenth century (theologians who are often typecast as villains or heroes on this issue, but often by individuals who have never considered the positions of those theologians at length). To cite one case where their work has been neglected to the detriment of the modern discussion, Princeton's Benjamin Warfield on several occasions distinguished between the autographic "codex" of Scripture (now lost) and the autographic "text" (substantially present in modern critical editions of the Greek and Hebrew manuscripts), a small distinction which nonetheless would end most of the protracted discussion about a supposedly missing "autograph" of the Bible.[1] I also happen to agree with the statement in Fisher Humphreys' chapter that "when inerrancy is qualified carefully, I am unable to detect any substantial differences between it and the high view of Scripture offered by many noninerrantists." And so in some sense, I feel that the word *inerrancy* gets in the way of progress on the question of the Bible's authority.

All this having been said, the issues surrounding the idea of biblical inerrancy are absolutely critical. No church survives as a healthy reflection of God's work which does not honor God's written word. Yet no church speaks responsibly to its world which does not interpret Scripture with all the possible resources at its disposal. So it is a pleasure to commend the arguments and information of *The Unfettered Word*, not necessarily because this book has the last word on its subject, but because it is presented with the intent to clarify those "sacred writings which are able to instruct you for salvation through faith in Christ Jesus" (2 Tim. 3:15 RSV).

1. For example, Warfield, "The Inerrancy of the Original Autographs," *The Independent*, March 23, 1893; as found in *Selected Shorter Writings of B. B. Warfield*, John E. Meeter, ed., 2 vols. (Phillipsburg, N.J.: Presbyterian and Reformed, 1970, 1973), II:580–87.

Preface

In this book, some of the best-known and best-prepared Southern Baptist scholars grapple with one of the most contested issues of the last hundred years. The issue they discuss is "the authority-inerrancy question," that is, the question about these two things and how they are related to each other: belief in the Bible's authority, and belief in the Bible's inerrancy (or "errorlessness").

That issue is the flash point in an eight-year-old struggle within America's largest Protestant denomination, the Southern Baptist Convention. So far as evangelicals are concerned, the importance of the struggle was assessed by Dr. Kenneth Kantzer, distinguished former editor of *Christianity Today.* To Southern Baptists he said in 1987, "You are the pace-setter for all evangelical bodies in the United States and, perhaps, in the world." What Southern Baptists do "sets the direction in which millions of others will go."[1]

What Is Different About This Book

At least four things make this book distinctive, besides the fact that it is written for laypeople, and has been kept free of unexplained technical terms.

1. *The book offers some fresh help on an issue faced by everyone who cares about the Bible.* Though inerrancy itself may not be an issue for some people, they almost certainly care about the truthfulness of the Bible.

1. Kenneth S. Kantzer, "Parameters of Biblical Inerrancy," *The Proceedings of the Conference on Biblical Inerrancy 1987*, Michael A. Smith, ed. (Nashville: Broadman, 1987), 111.

2. *The book treats its Baptist material as illustrative of problems which arise within every denomination, and within every thoughtful soul.*

The current issues and the historic background of the Southern Baptist controversy are brought out here. But there is nothing peculiarly Baptist about the biblical and theological issues treated in Parts One and Two. Accordingly, there are virtually no Baptist references in those parts of the book, apart from some footnotes to Southern Baptist scholarship.

In the second half of the book, when Baptist personalities and developments do claim attention, they are treated as vivid illustrations or incisive expressions of issues and ideas that are pertinent to everyone. Chapter titles and part titles highlight this side of the picture in Parts Three and Four.

3. *The book fills a surprising void in the Southern Baptist controversy.* What has been lacking is an integrated, book-length, scholarly discussion of the chief biblical issues from a moderate-conservative perspective.

By virtue of its "main thrust," this book fills that void. But I must point out with some emphasis that not all the book's authors agree with the main thrust of the book. A number can be described as inerrantists, or would insist upon being so described, though the majority are moderates or moderate-conservatives.

One reason it is important to fill the void in the current controversy[2] is that a one-sided and sometimes very misleading picture of the Baptist and Southern Baptist past has been inculcated in the 1980s by certain inerrantist books.[3]

2. Russell H. Dilday, Jr.'s scholarly little 1982 book is not a true precedent for this book. It presents a conservative Baptist understanding of biblical authority which does not depend upon strict "inerrancy," and it takes note of limits and dangers associated with the term. But counterbalancing statements are included. Cf. Russell H. Dilday, Jr., *The Doctrine of Biblical Authority* (Nashville: Convention Press, 1982), 55, 58–61, 98–101.

3. For example, the large and in many respects very helpful *Baptists and the Bible* (Chicago: Moody Press, 1980), by L. Russ Bush and Tom J. Nettles; and the widely disseminated *Authority: The Critical Issue for*

If Southern Baptists had consumed a balanced diet of their own history during this period, their struggle over the Bible would have had a rather different look by the latter 1980s.

"Editor's introductions" have been added to chapters in Parts Three and Four. Their purpose is to bring out the contemporary importance of the historical information presented there—for everyone, Baptist or non-Baptist—and also to show how controversy still swirls around these persons and ideas.

4. *Finally, the book has a number of important links with Southern Baptists' first large-scale effort to discuss the biblical issues.* That first major step toward talking rather than merely fighting was the 1987 Ridgecrest Conference on Biblical Inerrancy.

This Book and Ridgecrest 1987

From May 4–7, 1987, the presidents of the six Southern Baptist seminaries sponsored the conference at Ridgecrest, North Carolina. Over a thousand people attended.

Nine of the chapters in this book had already appeared at the time of the conference (in earlier and less complete versions). They were included in "Confronting the Bible," a series of articles in the monthly, *SBC Today.*[4] At Ridgecrest it became evident that some of these articles had had a significant impact on important ideas presented at the conference (see chapter 1).

Even more important, the chapters in this book as they now stand are full of implicit answers to things said at Ridgecrest.

Southern Baptists (Old Tappan, N. J.: Revell, 1984) by James T. Draper, Jr. Problems associated with these books are discussed in the editor's introductions to chapters 7–9.

4. Under the editing of Robison B. James, the series began as an announced monthly feature in the May 1986 issue. But in a broader sense, and without the title, the series began with an article by James in November 1985. The nine essays mentioned, chapters 2–9 and 11, appear here much revised and with full documentation added. Five of the nine are so thoroughly rewritten that they are essentially new essays (3, 6, 7, 9 and 11).

I bring out some of the most important connections of this sort in introductions to chapters 7 and 8.

In the final chapter, I try to capture the main significance of the Ridgecrest conference for the church in general, and for the Southern Baptist controversy in particular.

The Ridgecrest papers, now published as the *Proceedings* of the conference,[5] are an immensely valuable resource. Some of the essays are excellent. But they are uneven in quality, and their essentially unedited status and sheer bulk (554 very large pages!) are intimidating. The reader with limited time is likely to be overwhelmed without some kind of guide and perspective—such as this book provides, especially in chapter 12.

The Two Sides in the Controversy

When they were writing their chapters or introductions, several of the authors in this book had occasion to refer to the two sides in the Southern Baptist controversy. Sometimes they used the expressions "fundamental-conservative" and "moderate-conservative," terms which have been employed routinely by the denominational press since early 1986. The terms were introduced at that time by the respected chairman of a panel created in 1985 to mediate the dispute, the Southern Baptist Peace Committee.[6]

5. Michael A. Smith, ed., *Proceedings*, note 1 above.

6. Before the 1987 Southern Baptist Convention met, most of this book had already been written. It was conceived and has been written throughout in fullest agreement with the request subsequently made at that gathering that there be a spirit of reconciliation, and that inflammatory language be avoided. The terms "fundamental-conservative" and "moderate-conservative" were invented in order that Southern Baptists could talk about the realities of their situation while giving as little offense as possible. The terms remain in this book because there would be some question of "rewriting history," and some delay of the book, if they were deleted, and because no replacements for them seem available. For example, it could be misleading if fundamental-conservatives were simply called "conservatives." Large numbers of moderate-conservatives are also very conservative.

"Fundamental-conservatives" are those who sympathize with an effort that began in 1978 to redirect the agencies of Southern Baptists, including their six seminaries, by electing working majorities of strict inerrantists to the governing boards of those institutions.[7]

"Moderate-conservatives" are a more diverse group, including large numbers of inerrantists and other conservatives as well as moderates. They sympathize with the effort that commenced in late 1980 to oppose the fundamental-conservative plan.[8] Of course, the words also appear here in their usual senses, without the hyphen, as in the expression "moderate conservative."

A Believer's Book, a Believer's Question

The authors in this book are individuals of unabashed evangelical piety, and their commitment to the authority of Scripture is strong and deep. "In that case," some people will ask, "what are they doing, some of them, raising questions about biblical inerrancy?"

In the minds of many, authority and inerrancy have been welded so tightly together—usually by the flame of fiery preaching more than by the lamp of patient study—that any question about inerrancy sounds to them like an attempt to evade the Bible's authority, or to nullify it.[9]

But what if it is the other way around? What if *the nature and authority of the Bible itself* force the believer to back off from inerrancy, or to back off from some forms of inerrancy,

7. Houston Appeals Court Judge Paul Pressler, principal architect of the plan, was astonishingly frank about the details in a radio interview broadcast in July 1986. "Firestorm Chats," Dominion Tapes, P. O. Box 8204, Fort Worth, Texas 76124.

8. Claude L. Howe, Jr., "From Houston to Dallas: Recent Controversy in the Southern Baptist Convention," in *The Controversy in the Southern Baptist Convention*, Fisher Humphreys, ed. (New Orleans: Faculty of New Orleans Baptist Theological Seminary, 1985), 31–44; cf. 38, 39 especially.

9. The difference between authority and inerrancy is explored at length in chapter 6.

anyway? That is precisely the experience of many devout and honest people. In such cases, "the authority-inerrancy question" is anything but an unbeliever's question. It is a believer's question, asked by people who love and trust the Bible.

If that still seems strange, it may be that the reader is thinking of "authority" in a thin and unbiblical sense. Accepting the Bible's authority means much more than holding the Bible at arm's length and saying, "No mistakes in this book!" Accepting the Bible's authority means letting its contents invade one's life as one makes a commitment to be *true to* the Bible with one's whole heart and mind, in life and in death.

In that full-bodied sense of the term, the Bible's own authority impels some believers to raise questions about the strict inerrancy theory. They are not sure they can be *true* to the Bible, as God has given it, if they give their full allegiance to that particular view. They yield full allegiance of that kind only to the contents and claims of Scripture itself. For the Bible, not this or that view of it, is their authority.

This book is arranged so that a generally cumulative line of thought runs from chapter 2 through chapter 11. The several chapter and part titles should make this clear. Also, the Introduction presents a kind of recurring theme in the book. But, apart from these considerations, care has been taken so that the reader can begin with any of the chapters. This is especially true with respect to chapters 2–4 on the truthfulness of the Bible. These chapters are equally appropriate as follow-ups to the Introduction.

Research for the parts of this book authored by the editor, and the editing of the volume as a whole, were made possible by a semester's sabbatical leave and a summer research fellowship granted by the University of Richmond.

Robison B. James
August, 1987

The Authors

R. Alan Culpepper is professor of New Testament interpretation at The Southern Baptist Theological Seminary, Louisville, Kentucky, and editor of *Review and Expositor,* that faculty's theological journal. He chairs the steering committee for Literary Aspects of the Gospels Group of the Society of Biblical Literature. Among his five books is *Anatomy of the Fourth Gospel* (Fortress, 1983).

Russell H. Dilday, Jr., is president, Southwestern Baptist Theological Seminary, Fort Worth, Texas. He is author of *The Doctrine of Biblical Authority* (Convention Press, 1982). His 1960 doctoral dissertation at Southwestern was on the theology of E. Y. Mullins, who is the subject of his chapter in this book.

William R. Estep, Jr., is Distinguished Professor of Church History, Southwestern Baptist Theological Seminary, Fort Worth, Texas. Among his dozen books are *Renaissance and Reformation,* (Eerdmans, 1986), *The Reformation* (Broadman, 1979), and *The Anabaptist Story* (Eerdmans, 1975).

Fisher Humphreys is professor of theology, New Orleans (La.) Baptist Theological Seminary. He is editor of that faculty's journal, *The Theological Educator,* and of a special issue of that journal, *The Controversy in the Southern Baptist Convention* (1985), the first substantial, two-sided effort to document the controversy. His nine books include *The Nature of God* (Broadman, 1985) and *The Death of Christ* (Broadman, 1978).

Robison B. James is professor of religion at the University of Richmond in Virginia, and a former member (1976–1983) of the Virginia legislature. He is a contributing editor of the monthly *SBC Today,* and editor of "Confronting the Bible: The Baptist Adventure," a series of articles appearing in that journal. His thirty-five articles fall into the areas of theology, applied ethics, biblical interpretation, and denominational affairs.

Edgar V. McKnight is professor of religion at Furman University, Greenville, South Carolina. Among his books are *The Bible and the Reader* (Fortress, 1985), *Meaning in Texts* (Fortress, 1978—named Book of the Year by the Conference on Christianity and Literature), and *What Is Form Criticism?* (Fortress, 1969). His doctoral dissertation was on A. T. Robertson, the subject of his chapter in this book.

Thomas J. Nettles is associate professor of history, Mid-America Baptist Theological Seminary, Memphis, Tennessee, and chairman of its department of church history. His books include *By His Grace and for His Glory* (Baker Book House, 1986), *Growth for God's Glory* (Evans Press, 1980) and, as coauthor, *Baptists and the Bible* (Moody Press, 1980). He is associate editor of *Reformation Today.*

Stewart A. Newman is professor of philosophy, emeritus, Meredith College, in Raleigh, North Carolina. He was professor of philosophy of religion at Southeastern Baptist Theological Seminary, Wake Forest, North Carolina, 1952–1966, and at Southwestern Seminary, Fort Worth, Texas, 1939–1952. His 1964 book by Broadman Press, *W. T. Conner: Theologian of the Southwest,* is a biography of the man he treats in his chapter in this book.

Mark A. Noll is professor of history and church history, Wheaton (Ill.) College. One of his ten books is *Between Faith and Criticism: Evangelicals, Scholarship, and the Bible in America* (Harper & Row, 1986). Professors Noll and Pinnock, authors of the Foreword and Afterword, respectively, are the only non-Southern Baptist authors in the book.

Clark H. Pinnock is professor of systematic theology, McMaster Divinity College, Hamilton, Ontario (Canada). Two of his nine books are *The Scripture Principle* (Harper & Row, 1984) and *Biblical Revelation* (Moody Press, 1971).

Charles H. Talbert is professor of religion, Wake Forest University, Winston-Salem, North Carolina, and editor of the Society of Biblical Literature's Dissertation Series/New Testament. His books include *Reading Corinthians* (Crossroad, 1987), *Acts: Knox Preaching Guides* (John Knox Press, 1984), and *Reading Luke* (Crossroad, 1982).

1

Introduction

ROBISON B. JAMES

There is a story about Martin Luther which sums up beautifully what the Protestant Reformation was about. It also sums up what this book is about, and why it bears the title, *The Unfettered Word*.

As best we can tell, the year was 1503. Luther was twenty years old, and half way through his studies at the University of Erfurt. While browsing in the library, he came upon a copy of the Scriptures. The incident left a deep impression, apparently for two reasons. It was the first time Luther had ever had his hands on a complete Bible. And the Bible was chained.

In later life, Luther told how delighted he was to find the book. It contained so much more of the Gospels and Epistles than the lectionaries which were read in church week by week! As he turned the pages to the Old Testament, his eyes fell on the account of little Samuel and his mother Hannah. He read the story, entranced. "How fortunate I would be if I were to possess such a book!" he thought.[1]

Here was the man who would probably do more than any mortal since biblical times to *set the Bible free* so that people could read it, hear it, and heed it. And his first encounter with the Bible: What was it like? He discovered a chained book.

1. Luther's "Table Talk," comment dated November 1531, as cited in Willem Jan Kooiman, *Luther and the Bible,* John Schmidt, trans. (Philadelphia: Muhlenberg, 1961), 3. Some details of the story are not certain. For what I say about it, see pp. 1–9.

Later accounts of this episode were bound to embellish it. Some said Luther found the Bible tucked away, forgotten, and covered with thick dust. That is unlikely. Books were chained because they might be stolen. And that meant they were very valuable, or very much in use, or both.

Other versions of the story say the events took place after Luther became a monk in 1505, and that his superiors tried to keep him from reading the Bible. That is certainly wrong. When Luther entered the monastery, he was given a red leather copy of the Bible and admonished to read it industriously. Which he did.

The embellished versions of this story exaggerate the degree to which the Catholic church neglected the Bible at the time. And yet there is an authentic impulse here. "The chained Bible" captures something important. It is not that the Bible was so terribly neglected, though there was some of that. And it is not that the Bible was forbidden, for it was not.

No, the Bible which young Luther encountered was "chained" in the sense that it was hemmed in by certain preconceptions. So tightly did they bind the Scriptures that he had to devote years of study to the Bible before the Word broke free of its fetters and struck home in his heart with the liberating truth of a gracious God: that in Jesus Christ he justifies the sinner *through faith*.

Fetters Today?

Can we be at ease today because we have attained the "right view" of the Bible? Far from it. Only a surface understanding of the Bible would let us think the "chains" that bind it are the kinds of thing that *can* be broken, once and for all. We are constantly domesticating the Word, constantly becoming too comfortable with it, constantly imprisoning it in our neat systems of thought.

We fashion fetters for the Word each time we take our own beliefs about the Bible more seriously than we take what confronts us in the Bible itself. The challenge in every encounter with the Bible is to let it say what it wants to say, be what it really is, and mean what it honestly means— without boxing it in and shackling it with traditional interpretations or preconceptions.

What chains bind the Word today? There may be many, of course, but this book has a focus. Not all its authors agree, but a recurrent theme in these pages, a major thrust, so to speak, is as follows: Some forms of belief in biblical inerrancy become chains for many today, in much the same way as did the churchly traditions and preconceptions of Luther's day.

Simple Biblicism

What kinds of inerrancy belief fashion fetters for the Word today? *Not* the simple attitude of love and trust toward the Bible which we find in ordinary, faithful Christians. In a broad sense some of these people could be called "inerrantists." But the spontaneous, intuitive confidence they have in the Bible was a staple of the Christian church long before the term *inerrant* entered our language in the last century.[2]

The confidence in the Bible which these ordinary Christians feel is essentially an attitude of reverent readiness to believe what the Bible has to say, and to be faithful to it.

This attitude of rank-and-file believers does not shackle the Word. It is not a worked-out set of ideas which dictates, ahead of time, how the Bible must speak, and how we must interpret it.

Of course, these ordinary Christians have "working beliefs" according to which they use their Bibles day by day. These working beliefs, though largely unconscious, are flexible. They certainly are not "codified." The most notable is the belief that the New Testament provides a final word over what we sometimes find in the Old. The flexibility we see in

---

2. Paul D. Feinberg, "The Meaning of Inerrancy," in *Inerrancy*, Norman L. Geisler, ed. (Grand Rapids: Zondervan, 1980), 291, 292.

these working beliefs, and their openness to diversity in the Bible, make the simple approach *less* like the strict inerrancy view, not *more* like it.[3]

One of the most illuminating statements which has been made in the current Southern Baptist controversy was made by a non-Southern Baptist, Canadian theologian Clark Pinnock. Speaking at the 1987 Ridgecrest conference on inerrancy, Pinnock distinguished two approaches to the Bible. He labeled them "simple biblicism" and "elaborate" or "strict" inerrancy, respectively. It is his simple biblicism I have been describing, of course.

In an interview at the time, Pinnock commented that these two ideas were "new categories" in his thinking. He also noted that some of the stimulus for conceiving the issue in these terms came from the present author's contrast between "spontaneous" and "systematic" inerrancy, a contrast I present in chapter 6.[4] Of course, calling these categories "new" could be misleading. They are fresh attempts to retrieve something that is very, very old.

Another of the principal speakers at the Ridgecrest conference provided independent confirmation of Pinnock's two categories. Mark Noll's "Baptist way" of upholding a fully truthful Bible is the same pietist approach as Pinnock's "simple biblicism. Noll distinguished it sharply from the "Princeton Presbyterians'" approach. The latter, as we shall see, is the clearest example of Pinnock's elaborate view.[5]

3. In my "Baptist Faith and Message Statement: Best Answer," *SBC Today* 4 (October 1986), 8, 9, I give illustrations of several "working beliefs" according to which ordinary believers actually use their Bibles day in and day out, working beliefs that are inconsistent with strict, systematic inerrancy doctrine.
4. Interview of May 7, 1987. Pinnock had access to the "spontaneous-systematic" contrast in two of my articles in the series discussed in the Preface, namely, in "Biblical Authority or Inerrancy?," *SBC Today*, 3 (November 1985), 2, 6, 7, and "Believing the Bible Biblically," *SBC Today*, 4 (January 1987), 6, 7.
5. Mark A. Noll, "A Brief History of Inerrancy, Mostly in America," in Michael A. Smith, ed., *Proceedings of the Conference on Biblical*

The question at the Ridgecrest conference, Pinnock noted in an address there, is:

> whether it is prudent to insist upon a position of great elaboration and strictness with regard to the presuppositions with which we come to Scripture, or whether to adopt a simpler more spontaneous biblicism which also trusts the Bible without reservation but does not believe it is good to burden the Bible reader with too much human theory lest he or she miss what God is saying in the text. After all, presuppositions can distract us from seeing what lies before our very eyes.[6]

This simple biblicism, Pinnock explained, is the approach taken by most evangelicals and Baptists, whether scholars or not. It is a "Spirit-engendered inclination to love and trust the Scriptures." It "views the Scriptures as the only place to go to if you want to find the words of everlasting life." It is "the simple uncomplicated approach to the Bible which the Christian faith has always had. It seems to me," he added, "that 98 percent of Southern Baptists are simple biblicists, pietists rather than doctrinalists in their orientation."[7]

Elaborate or Strict Inerrancy

By contrast with this simple approach, there is "inerrancy" properly so called. Historically, said Pinnock, "biblical inerrancy . . . is a term belonging to the grammar and vocabulary of strict orthodoxy." It was developed among Protestants who hoped, "by framing their theory of inspiration on a high level of technical precision," that they could preserve the truth of Scripture from distortion, and protect the flock of God from unbelief.[8]

On the American scene, the most pivotal articulation of the elaborate theory is the "Princeton theology." A classic document of that view, still perhaps its most definitive single

---

Inerrancy 1987 (Nashville: Broadman, 1987), 13–19. Cf. Clark Pinnock, "What Is Biblical Inerrancy?," in *Proceedings*, 75.

6. Ibid.
7. Ibid.
8. Ibid., 76.

statement, is a long 1881 article entitled "Inspiration," written by the Princeton Presbyterians, A. A. Hodge and B. B. Warfield.[9]

One of the most familiar complexities of the elaborate theory is the way scholarly inerrantists *qualify* what they mean when they say the Bible is inerrant. Fisher Humphreys explains eleven qualifications of this sort in chapter 4. A shorter list, purely illustrative, is this: It is not the copies of the Bible we now have, but the original manuscripts that are inerrant; it is not what may have been thought or assumed by the biblical writer that is inerrant, but what is *intended to be affirmed*, either by the writer or by God or by the text; and (for some inerrantists), it is not what the Bible says, but what it *means to teach* that is inerrant.

And, further, it is not an error when the following things happen: when events are narrated out of chronological order;[10] when numbers in different accounts of the same event differ;[11] when the Gospels say Jesus said this or that, and then give his general sense, but not his actual words; and when biblical writers attribute statements to other parts of the Bible, but quote them loosely and inexactly (not intending to give the words as in the original, the authors made no error).

The preceding points are made, not by critics of strict

9. A. A. Hodge and B. B. Warfield, "Inspiration," *Presbyterian Review*, II (April 1881), 225–260. With an introduction, notes and appendices, it has been republished as *Inspiration*, edited by Roger R. Nicole (Grand Rapids: Baker, 1979). Cf. also Mark A. Noll, ed., *The Princeton Theology 1812–1921* (Phillipsburg, N. J.: Presbyterian and Reformed Publishing Co., 1983).

10. For example, Mark says Jesus cursed the fig tree the day he cleansed the temple, whereas Matthew says he cursed it the morning after; but there is no error according to this view, because at least one of them had no intention of affirming a sequence of events when he said, "The next day" (Mark 11:12) or "he left them and went out to the city to Bethany, where he spent the night. Early in the morning, as he was on his way back to the city . . ." (Matt. 21:17, 18).

11. At least in the following seven places, the numbers in the parallel Chronicles account are very different from the numbers in 2 Sam. 8:4; 10:6, 18; 24:24; 1 Kings 4:26; 6:2, and 7:26. E.g., Solomon's temple was thirty or one hundred twenty cubits in height.

inerrancy, of course, but by advocates[12]—advocates who are recognized as leading inerrantist authorities by (for example) the most prominent of Southern Baptist fundamental-conservatives.[13]

On its face, an elaborate inerrancy view is far more likely to "fetter the Word" than simple biblicism is. But is that what strict inerrancy does?

People differ. Personalities differ. To some people, something like the strict inerrancy view may appear to be a necessity for their spiritual health, if not for their spiritual life itself. It is hoped that the Word will nevertheless show its capacity to be more than they had expected, free in surprising ways to be more fully itself for them.

For a great many other people, however, strict inerrancy puts fetters on the Word in a direct and oppressive way. Two examples: (1) Most Baptists and evangelicals are pietist rather than doctrinalist. For them, the determined effort to *conform their own thinking* to strict inerrancy "cuts against the grain," the God-given grain, of their spiritual lives. They realize, as Saul of Tarsus realized, that *they* are not free. But they do not realize that the Word is not free, and that they will not be free until it is. (2) Advocates of strict inerrancy are very apt to try to impose their view on others. They do this either by attempting to enforce a creedal statement on denominational leaders, or by stirring up and unleashing a kind of "peer pressure" on everybody. Their motive in doing this is worthy.

12. Cf. Hodge and Warfield, "Inspiration," 237, 238, 245, 246, and Art. 13 of the 1978 Chicago Statement, in N. L. Geisler, ed., *Inerrancy*, 496.

13. At the Ridgecrest conference, five of the six visiting inerrantists dealt with this issue of "qualifications." They indicated agreement with the qualifications I have listed, except that some of them would demur on the qualification concerning "what the Bible means to teach." Michael A. Smith, ed., *Proceedings*, 51–55, 75–77, 114–118, 177–188, 210–213. Top leaders among fundamental-conservative Southern Baptists were present and expressed their agreement with these scholars: Paige Patterson, Adrian Rogers, and H. Edwin Young, for example. Ibid., 65, 125, 146.

They want to be sure *the Bible rules*. But that is not what happens.

Rather, the proper ruling position of the Bible is usurped. It is usurped by a creedalized view *about* the Bible—and also by groups of powerful individuals who are determined that no one shall be allowed recourse to Scripture *apart* from that creedal view of the Bible. Apart from that view of it, the Bible is a book *forbidden to be used*, at least for anyone who seeks to lead in the denomination. The Word is fettered.

That sounds negative in a way this book is not. Some of the chapters in this book show how this fettering of the Word comes about, yes. But it is more important that these chapters show, in a thoroughly positive way, how we may deal with the Bible so that such problems *need not arise*.

The hope lying behind this book recalls the story of young Luther with which this chapter began. It is the hope that something Luther read that day will be true today—that each time the reader turns to Scripture, the reader will be able to say, as did the boy Samuel, "Speak, Lord, for your servant is listening" (1 Sam. 3:9).

PART ONE
THE TRUTHFULNESS OF THE BIBLE

2

Jesus' View of Scripture

R. ALAN CULPEPPER

On one assertion about the Bible most Christians (and all Southern Baptists) can agree: "The criterion by which the Bible is to be judged is Jesus Christ."[1]

We understand and interpret the message of Scripture in light of the revelation in Jesus. Our understanding of Scripture itself, therefore, should be informed and shaped by Jesus' view of Scripture. The way in which the New Testament answers the following questions will, therefore, form a secure biblical foundation for our own understanding of the nature of Scripture:

1. What did Jesus say about Scripture?
2. How did Jesus use Scripture?
3. Did Jesus believe in the inerrancy of Scripture?

On the basis of relevant passages in the Gospels, answers can be found to the first two questions. Because the word *inerrancy* does not appear anywhere in the Bible, however, the third question must be answered by comparing Jesus' view of Scripture with the theory of inerrancy. Each of these questions is taken up below.

What Did Jesus Say About Scripture?

Although the Scriptures are quoted and referred to many times in the Gospels, Jesus had remarkably little to say about

---

1. The assertion comes from Article 1 of The Baptist Faith and Message, the confession of faith adopted by the Southern Baptist Convention in 1963.

the nature of Scripture. Undoubtedly he accepted the authority of Scripture as the record of God's revelation to man, as did other pious Jews of his time. Jesus taught from the Scriptures (Luke 24:27, 32, 45), but much of the time he chose to tell parables instead. Jesus affirmed the divine authority of Scripture: "'Have you not read what God said to you . . .'" (Matt. 22:31). He taught that Scripture was fulfilled through his ministry (Matt. 26:54, 56).

On the other hand, Jesus did not enter into debates about the authority of Scripture in matters that did not concern salvation, God's redemptive work, or mankind's relationship to God.

Matthew 5:18 is a key verse. Here Jesus affirms the authority of Scripture even as he prepares to redefine that authority in relation to his own teaching. In a taped and widely circulated lecture entitled "Jesus and the Word,"[2] the president of Criswell College, Dr. Paige Patterson, uses Matthew 5:18 as the biblical basis for arguing that Jesus believed in the inerrancy of Scripture. In fact, that verse contains a claim of Jesus' superior authority and introduces a series of six statements in which Jesus demands a standard of righteousness higher than that set by the Hebrew Scriptures and the traditions of the Pharisees. Matthew 5:18 reads:

> For truly, I say to you, till heaven and earth pass away, not an iota, not a dot, will pass from the law until all is accomplished. (RSV)

Patterson correctly explains that an "iota," or "jot," is the smallest letter of the Hebrew alphabet and a "dot," or "tittle" is a tiny hook or projection that is required to make certain letters. He does not point out, however, that this verse is introduced by a reference to Jesus' personal authority, "For truly, I say to you. . . ." Neither does he explain that whatever Matthew 5:18 means, it cannot be taken to mean that the

---

2. "Dr. Paige Patterson—Biblical Inerrancy," taped lecture, distributed by Latimer House, Box 330205, Fort Worth, Texas 76163–0205.

Law and the Prophets would remain eternally binding. Jesus came not to destroy the Law and the Prophets but to bring them to fulfillment (Matt. 5:17). The Law and the Prophets would never have the kind of unparalleled authority among Christians that they had among the scribes and the Pharisees. Jesus was not "relaxing" the commandments (Matt. 5:19); he was calling for a higher standard of righteousness while promising unlimited grace.

The first of the six antitheses follows: "'You have heard that is was said to the people long ago, "Do not murder. . . ." But I tell you that anyone who is angry with his brother will be subject to judgment'" (Matt. 5:21, 22). Here Jesus quotes from the Ten Commandments (Exod. 20:13; Deut. 5:17) and then proceeds to give a new teaching on his own authority.

In response to such radical freedom, the crowds marveled and the authorities conspired against him. Matthew 5:18, therefore, is easily misinterpreted if it is not interpreted in the context of verses 21–48. As usual, New Testament scholar Frank Stagg puts the matter clearly:

> Verse 18 is not to be so interpreted as to contradict Jesus' own refusal to be bound by a wooden, literal reading of Scripture. This verse may best be understood as his protest against the disposition to set aside the Law. Jesus made what appears to be an extreme statement. His own actions and teachings demonstrate that he always took Scripture seriously but not always literally. To literalize may be to trivialize. Jesus is not a neo-legalist, making the letter of the Law supreme. His own *I say to you* shows that he stood above the Law, not it above him.[3]

Matthew 5:18, therefore, can be used to support the theory of inerrancy only by taking it in isolation from Matthew 5:21–48, which it introduces.

Perhaps we should be careful about making a dogma of the inerrancy of Scripture or about defining our understanding of

---

3. Frank Stagg, "Matthew," *Broadman Bible Commentary*, vol. 8 (Nashville: Broadman Press, 1969), 107, 108.

the nature of Scripture on the basis of the original manuscripts, no longer extant. Nowhere in the New Testament
does Jesus ever refer to "inerrancy" or to "original autographs."[4] *Jesus said nothing about inerrancy.* In fact, he said
nothing about the inspiration of Scripture.

Neither does the Bible itself define the authority of Scripture in terms of the inerrancy of the original autographs (see
2 Tim. 3:16; 2 Pet. 1:20, 21). The Bible affirms that Scripture
is inspired and authoritative, "useful for teaching, rebuking,
correcting, and training in righteousness" (2 Tim. 3:16); but
it says nothing about inerrancy or original autographs.

How Did Jesus Use Scripture?

In his taped lecture, Patterson ignores those passages in
which Jesus demonstrates a radical freedom from the teachings of Scripture and sets his own authority above that of the
Hebrew Scriptures. Of course Jesus believed in the Scriptures and defended their authority, but he also exercised a
freedom from them that was so radical that the religious
authorities of his day conspired to kill him.

Hearing Patterson, one would think that no rabbi ever had
a higher regard for the authority of Scripture in every detail
than Jesus himself. Why then did the authorities reject him
and crucify him? The Gospels leave no doubt: the authorities
conspired against Jesus because he violated the Law of Moses
and put his own authority above Scripture. The religious authorities also persecuted the early Christians for speaking
"'blasphemy against Moses and against God'" (Acts 6:11).

A few *examples of Jesus' radical freedom from the com-
mands of Scripture* will suffice. When Jesus healed on the
sabbath, he violated the command to observe the sabbath, at
least as it was commonly understood:

4. Everett F. Harrison, "The Phenomena of Scripture," in *Revelation
and the Bible*, Carl F. H. Henry, ed. (Grand Rapids: Baker Book House,
1958), 238: "One must grant that the Bible itself, in advancing its own
claim of inspiration, says nothing precise about inerrancy. This remains a
conclusion to which devout minds have come because of the divine character of Scripture."

And this was why the Jews persecuted Jesus, because he did this on the sabbath. . . . This was why the Jews sought all the more to kill him, because he not only broke the sabbath but also called God his Father, making himself equal with God.

(John 5:16, 18 RSV)

The Gospel of Mark records a similar healing and makes the same point. Jesus met a man with a withered hand. While the authorities watched to see whether Jesus would heal him on the sabbath, Jesus challenged them, "'Which is lawful on the Sabbath: to do good or to do evil, to save life or to kill?'" (3:4). Grieved at their hardness of heart, Jesus healed the man. But the Pharisees "went out and began to plot with the Herodians how they might kill Jesus" (3:6). For Jesus, meeting human needs took precedence even over the command to observe the sabbath: "'The Sabbath was made for man, not man for the Sabbath'" (Mark 2:27).

Similarly, when Jesus was asked about divorce he answered by stating the divine purpose for marriage. The Pharisees then asked why Moses (i.e., Deut. 24: 1, 3) permitted divorce, requiring only that the divorced woman be given a certificate. Jesus responded by dismissing this part of Scripture:

"For your hardness of heart Moses allowed you to divorce your wives, but from the beginning it was not so. *And I say to you:* whoever divorces his wife, except for unchastity, and marries another, commits adultery."   (Matt. 19:8 RSV)

Jesus asserted his own authority over Scripture in a way that was intolerable to the religious authorities of his day. He altered the meaning of sabbath observance, and he rejected the provision for divorce in the Law of Moses.

At times the argument is raised that Jesus' references to persons or events in the Old Testament certify that he believed in the inerrancy of Scripture in every historical detail.[5]

---

5. John W. Wenham, "Christ's View of Scripture," *Inerrancy*, ed., Norman L. Geisler (Grand Rapids: Zondervan, 1980), 6, 7.

Actually, *when Jesus referred to events and persons described in the Scriptures, he was not making any judgment about the inerrancy of the biblical account.* Jesus neither questioned the accuracy of the accounts nor did he insist on it. As James Barr observes,

> Jesus took Jewish scripture as it was, as his contemporaries did, and he used it as they did in this respect, as a source through which authoritative intimations of divine truth had been given. Thus if Jesus refers to a passage in Exodus or in Deuteronomy with the words "Moses said," it is quite mistaken to read this as if he was placing his own full messianic and divine authority behind the assertion that these books were actually written by the historical Moses. No such question entered his head and there is nothing in the Gospels that suggests that his teaching was intended to cope with it. Historical questions interested him little.[6]

The force of Jesus' appeals to Scripture is diminished, not enhanced, by treating them as certifying matters of traditional authorship or historical accuracy. Jesus was concerned that people not tithe "mint, dill and cummin" while neglecting "the more important matters of the law—justice, mercy and faithfulness" (Matt. 23:23). Jesus was concerned with the inspired revelation in matters of life and obedience, faith and doctrine, not inerrancy in assertions regarding historical chronology, botany, geography, or astronomy.

When Jesus quoted the Scriptures, his words did not always agree with those of the Old Testament. It is painful to have to make such a point because the more significant observation is that Jesus knew the Scriptures thoroughly and cited them frequently. Jesus' use of the Scriptures, however, does not show that he was concerned to establish their inerrancy. When Jesus defended his disciples for plucking grain on the sabbath, he said:

6. James Barr, *Beyond Fundamentalism* (Philadelphia: Westminster Press, 1984), 11.

"Have you never read what David did, when he was in need
and was hungry . . . how he entered the house of God, when
Abiathar was high priest, and ate the bread of the Presence
. . . ?"   (Mark 2:25, 26 RSV)

The incident to which Jesus was referring did not happen
during the time of Abiathar, however, but involved his lesser
known father, Ahimelech (1 Sam. 21:1–6). Similarly, Jesus
warned the scribes and the Pharisees that all the righteous
blood shed on earth would come upon them, "'from the blood
of innocent Abel to the blood of Zechariah the son of
Barachiah, whom you murdered between the sanctuary and
the altar'" (Matt. 23:35 italics added). Second Chronicles
24:20, 21 records, however, that the murdered priest was
Zechariah the son of *Jehoiada*.

These are insignificant details which do not affect the inspiration and authority of Scripture, but they do prove that
Jesus did not use the Scriptures inerrantly. The same can be
said of the use of the Scriptures by the writers of the Gospels.
Mark 1:1–3 cites Isaiah, but part of the quotation comes from
Malachi 3:1 or Exodus 23:20.[7] The text that is quoted in
Luke 4:18 is a blending of Isaiah 61:1 and Isaiah 58:6. Jesus
did not cite the Old Testament inerrantly; neither did the
evangelists.

Finally, *Jesus pointed the Jews beyond Scripture to its fulfillment in himself.* He chided the Jews for thinking that
eternal life was to be found in the Scriptures, yet refusing to
believe in him (John 5:39, 40). Unless one sees that the
Scriptures point to Jesus, one has not understood them and
they remain powerless to give life. Isaiah 61 was fulfilled, but
the synagogue at Nazareth did not recognize its fulfillment.

In his fulfillment of Scripture, moreover, Jesus set aside
the cultic and ritual law of the old covenant (Mark 7:19). He

7. A footnote at this point in the Living Bible merely shows the im-
possibility of reconciling the data of the biblical text with the theory of
inerrancy.

reinterpreted the law regarding divorce (Matt. 19:8). And, rather than a new set of writings that would be inerrant or legally binding he promised the Holy Spirit that would teach his disciples all things (John 14:25, 26).

What conclusion can we draw from Jesus' use and teachings about the Scriptures?

Did Jesus Believe in the Inerrancy of Scripture?

The current power struggle in the Southern Baptist Convention is representative of a larger controversy among Protestants about the Bible. Both among Baptists and in the broader arena, some have chosen to make belief in the inerrancy of Scripture a test of fellowship. Arguments have been mounted to defend both the moderate and the fundamentalist positions.

Moderates have claimed that "the Scriptures of the Old and New Testaments were given by inspiration of God, and are the only sufficient, certain and authoritative rule of all *saving* knowledge, faith and obedience," as The Abstract of Principles of the Southern Baptist Theological Seminary, adopted in 1858, states it (Article 1).

On the other hand, inerrantists have insisted that others within their denomination must also affirm that the "original autographs" of the books of the Bible were *inerrant,* meaning that they were without error in all matters—history, science, geography, or mathematics.

While this costly debate has raged over the past decade (diverting attention from the organized political takeover of the Southern Baptist Convention), inerrantists have sought to defend their view of the Bible by arguing that Jesus was an inerrantist.

No one can quarrel with the rightness of looking to the teachings of Jesus for guidance in defining our understanding of Scripture. But, was Jesus an inerrantist, as some have recently claimed? Before the question can be answered, the issue must be stated clearly.

The issue is whether Jesus was an inerrantist. The issue is not whether Jesus believed in the inspiration and authority of Scripture. Of course he did. Lacking evidence to deal with the specific issue of inerrancy, those who have argued that Jesus was an inerrantist have obscured the issue.

Arguments that Jesus quoted Scripture as reliable doctrine, or that he believed in the inspiration and authority of Scripture—which of course are all true—do not demonstrate that Jesus believed in the inerrancy of Scripture. Before we can answer the question, "was Jesus an inerrantist?" we must be clear about what is meant by "inerrancy."

The Chicago Statement on Biblical Inerrancy, drafted following a meeting sponsored by the International Council on Biblical Inerrancy (or ICBI) in 1978, gave the term a rather general and bland definition but then attached to it several qualifications. Inerrancy, it declared,

> signifies the quality of being free from all falsehood or mistake and so safeguards the truth that Holy Scripture is entirely true and trustworthy *in all its assertions.*[8]

Taken by itself this is a statement around which one could find much agreement among moderates and fundamentalists alike. The Chicago Statement itself takes the edge off of this statement by conceding that

> Since, for instance, non-chronological narration and imprecise citation were conventional and acceptable and violated no expectations in those days, we must not regard these things as faults when we find them in the Bible writers. When total precision of a particular kind is not expected nor aimed at, it is no error not to have achieved it. Scripture is inerrant, not in the sense of being absolutely precise by modern standards, but in

8. "The Chicago Statement on Inerrancy," International Council on Biblical Inerrancy, Chicago, Illinois, October 26–28, 1978, published in *Inerrancy,* ed., Norman L. Geisler (Grand Rapids: Zondervan, 1980), 500 (emphasis mine).

the sense of making good its claims and achieving that measure of focused truth at which its authors aimed.[9]

We are left in hopeless contradictions. How can we be guided by the literal meaning of Scripture, claim that it is free from mistake "in all its assertions," and yet recognize that Scripture is not "absolutely precise"?

Where contradiction or "imprecision" cannot be dismissed, the customary response is to claim that only the original manuscripts or "autographs" of each book of the Bible were inerrant. Yet, none of these original manuscripts have survived. Moreover, there are differences in accounts of the same event at points even where variant readings among the fifty-five hundred Greek manuscripts of the New Testament do not solve the problem.

For example, was Jesus crucified after the Passover meal (Mark 14:12, 16) or before (John 18:28; 19:14)? Did Judas hang himself (Matt. 27:5) or fall and burst open (Acts 1:18)?

These are obviously minor points, but if we must assume that there were no discrepancies at these points in the original manuscripts, then we must also conclude that our present manuscripts are in error and that we do not have any evidence as to what the original autographs said at these points.

Ultimately, therefore, the appeal to the "original autographs" serves only to undermine confidence in the many fine manuscripts of the Bible that we do possess, and on which all modern translations depend.

Faced with these difficulties, Baptists and other Protestants have traditionally affirmed the inspiration and authority of Scripture in all *saving* knowledge, rather than attempting to defend inerrancy in all that the Bible asserts. Inerrantists, however, refuse to accept such a distinction.

John Wenham, for example, in a publication sponsored by the ICBI, rejects the claim that "Scripture is factually true and authoritative in all matters 'crucially relevant to Christian

9. Ibid., 500, 501.

faith and practice,' but not in peripheral matters." Instead, Wenham argues that "the attempt to discriminate between the crucial and the peripheral appears to be a product of the nineteenth and twentieth centuries."[10]

However, evangelicals in this country—and not least the largest Protestant group, Southern Baptists—are now divided over precisely this issue. The crucial difference between two groups which have been called, respectively, "moderate-conservatives" and "fundamental-conservatives," is exposed by their interpretations of a statement from The Baptist Faith and Message, Southern Baptists' 1963 confession of faith.

> The Holy Bible was written by men divinely inspired and is the record of God's revelation of Himself to man. It is a perfect treasure of divine instruction. It has God for its author, salvation for its end, and truth, without mixture of error, for its matter. . . . The criterion by which the Bible is to be interpreted is Jesus Christ.

Moderate conservatives recognize the limitation present within the phrase "for its matter." Dr. Hugh Wamble, professor of church history at Midwestern Baptist Theological Seminary, has traced this statement to a personal letter written by the philosopher John Locke on August 25, 1703.[11] Locke may have been quoting a statement that did not originate with him. At the time it was customary to distinguish between form and matter. "Form" meant the verbal expression, grammar, style, or literary character of Scripture. "Matter" designated its essential content.

Thus, declaring that the Bible has truth *for its matter* affirms that the Bible contains all truth—"without mixture of error"—regarding matters of faith and doctrine.

This distinction is made in other confessions also. The

10. Wenham, "Christ's View of Scripture," 22.
11. G. Hugh Wamble, "Locke Confesses 'Truth without Error,'" *Western Recorder* (September 16, 1986), 8, citing *The Works of John Locke*, vol. 10.

Abstract of Principles of the Southern Baptist Seminary states, "The Scriptures . . . are the only sufficient, certain and authoritative rule of all *saving* knowledge, faith and obedience."

Both the Abstract of Principles and The Baptist Faith and Message, therefore, confine their claims to the "matter" of the Bible, "saving knowledge, faith and obedience," making no claims regarding other areas, such as science and history.

The fundamental-conservatives, of course, are not satisfied with these historic confessions. Instead, they demand that affirmations about the authority of Scripture be extended to cover its accuracy "in all its assertions." Another part of the Chicago Statement (Article 12) shows how different the position of inerrancy is from that contained in the confessions we have just examined:

> We deny that Biblical infallibility and inerrancy are limited to spiritual, religious, or redemptive themes, exclusive of assertions in the fields of history and science.[12]

The claims of inerrancy go far beyond what the Bible claims for itself, and far beyond what Southern Baptists and other Protestants have affirmed in their historic confessions. *Inerrancy is a modern theory regarding the accuracy of the original manuscripts of the Bible in matters that are irrelevant to its essential message.*

The issue, therefore, is not whether Jesus affirmed the reliability of the Scriptures in matters of saving knowledge, faith, and doctrine, but whether he affirmed the inerrancy of the Scriptures—or their original autographs, about which Jesus said nothing—in all other matters as well.

In responding to the argument that Jesus was an inerrantist, it is important to bear in mind four points that have been documented in this chapter:

12. Geisler, *Inerrancy*, 496.

1. Jesus never referred to the "inerrancy" of Scripture or to "original autographs."

2. Jesus showed little concern for the historical accuracy of the Old Testament.

3. Jesus did not handle the Scriptures inerrantly.

4. Jesus pointed the Jews beyond Scripture to its fulfillment in himself.

Did Jesus guard and teach the Scriptures as the inspired, authoritative record of God's revelation? Certainly he did. Jesus used the Scriptures to guide those whom he taught in matters of saving knowledge, faith, and doctrine. But, he did not appeal to the Scriptures as an authority in other matters. Jesus did not teach inerrancy.

3

The Bible's Truth Is Relational

CHARLES H. TALBERT

What does one listen for in a dialogue with the Bible? That is, what kind of assistance is the Bible intended and divinely qualified to give?

For me, the Bible speaks with authority on relational or soteriological (salvational) matters, not necessarily on incidental matters of fact. I am aware this is the dividing line between myself and many of my Christian friends. It is a matter that needs to be addressed even among friends, however. I aim to do that briefly here.

What the Bible Means to Say

Let me begin with an analogy. We had met, dated, and made commitments. Then she went off to another state to teach for a year. I planned a trip to see her. Before I left, her letter arrived, telling me three things: (a) something of the history of the school; (b) how to get there, especially the last stretch, which was on state roads; and (c) that she loved me, still wanted to marry me and was eager for me to arrive.

Before I left, I read the school catalog and saw it was not founded in exactly the year the letter said. It was close, but not exact. The letter was exactly right about why the school was founded. Before I left, I also checked the highways with a state map, including the state roads. All was correct about the directions in the letter except, when I reached the final crossroads, I needed to turn right instead of left. Just that one detail of geography was out of place.

When I arrived she was truly thrilled to see me. She said

she did want to get married and we set the date. In our general relating to one another, there was no doubt in my mind that she loved me. I had the relational data in the letter verified by experience with her. The factual data I checked against other sources, finding most things accurate but a couple of items slightly off target.

So it is when I listen to the Bible. The Bible is an acknowledged expert in the relational data (how God relates to me, how I am related to God, to others, to myself, to the world). Moreover, these truths are validated by my experience with God. Matters of history and science I check against other sources to determine their accuracy. Inaccuracies in incidental matters of fact do not detract from relational truth that is validated in experience.

This I take to be the intent of the 1858 Abstract of Principles of The Southern Baptist Theological Seminary, the first statement of faith adopted by an institution associated with the Southern Baptist Convention. In Article 1, "The Scriptures," it says:

> The Scriptures of the Old and New Testaments were given by inspiration of God and are the only sufficient, certain and authoritative rule of all *saving* knowledge, faith and obedience (italics mine).

This view is by no means peculiar to Baptists, however, or even to Protestants. In Section 11 of "The Constitution on Revelation" from the Second Vatican Council (1962–1965), we read,

> . . . the books of Scripture must be acknowledged as teaching firmly, faithfully and without error that truth which God wanted put in the sacred writings *for the sake of our salvation* (italics mine).

A Different View

A position such as I have described runs directly counter to the view taken by the International Council on Biblical Inerrancy, or ICBI, which was founded in 1977. In its 1978

"Chicago Statement on Biblical Inerrancy," the ICBI says the following:

> We deny that biblical infallibility and inerrancy are limited to spiritual, religious, or redemptive themes exclusive of assertions in the fields of history and science.[1]

In the "Short Statement" preceding the detailed arguments of this 1978 document, the following is asserted:

> Scripture is without error . . . in all its teaching, no less in what it states about God's acts in creation, about its own literary origins under God, than in its witness to God's saving grace in individual lives.

In a recent interview, John R. W. Stott commented, "Simply to say that the Bible is inerrant may be misleading because there are things *contained* in the Bible that are not *affirmed* by the Bible. . . . What does it affirm in Genesis 1, 2, and 3? Is it affirming that the world, the universe was made in six days or not? So we have to argue about the hermeneutical question."[2]

Inerrantists argue that the Bible not only contains, but also affirms things about science, history, and geography. My contention is that the Scriptures affirm matters soteriological, not matters scientific, geographical, and historical, except as these latter things are inextricably related to its soteriological (or salvational) claims.

In the ICBI's second Chicago Statement of 1982, Article 6 reiterates the view we are discussing in the following words:

> We deny that, while Scripture is able to make us wise unto salvation, biblical truth should be defined in terms of this function.[3]

---

1. The 1978 ICBI statement is found in Norman L. Geisler, ed., *Inerrancy* (Grand Rapids: Zondervan, 1979), 493–497. The first quotation above is from Article 12 of the statement.

2. "The Church in the Modern World," *Mission Journal*, 19 (October 1985): 3–7 (italics mine).

3. *Hermeneutics, Inerrancy, and the Bible*, Earl D. Radmacher and Robert D. Preus, ed. (Grand Rapids: Zondervan, 1984), 892.

J. I. Packer's views are pertinent at this point. He follows the Protestant reformers' insight and contends that the Bible's authority is grounded in God's ability to speak through it, disclosing himself and bringing redemption. Thus the meaning of inerrancy is not determined ahead of time, a priori, but is formulated after we have encountered the Bible, listened to it, and let it show us its primary intent and purpose: salvation.[4] Thus, even though Packer is a member of the executive council of the ICBI, he is close to a position which the ICBI's statements are drawn up to exclude, the position of Jack B. Rogers.[5]

The contrasting views I am tracing here are epitomized in two books. One is dually authored by Jack Rogers and Donald McKim who argue that historically the church has asserted the infallibility of the Bible for faith and practice, but not inerrancy in matters of science, history, and geography.[6] The other book is by John Woodbridge, who takes the view set forth in the ICBI statements. Woodbridge refuses to accept the distinction made by Rogers and McKim, and claims rather that in church history the central tradition has held both to the infallibility of the saving message, and to the inerrancy of the Bible in matters of fact as well.[7]

Jesus and the Old Testament

The insistence on extending the Bible's authority beyond the realm of religion into the spheres of science, geography, and history is sometimes focused on Jesus' words about the Old Testament. The 1978 ICBI statement says, in Article 15:

4. J. I. Packer, "Hermeneutics and Biblical Authority," *Themelios*, 1 (1975): 3–12; and J. I. Packer, *Fundamentalism and the Word of God* (Grand Rapids: Eerdmans, 1972), 94–101.

5. Article 16 of the 1978 ICBI statement says, "We deny that inerrancy is a doctrine invented by Scholastic Protestantism. . . ." The latter is a point Rogers makes, e.g., in *The Authority and Interpretation of the Bible*, 187, 188.

6. Jack B. Rogers and Donald K. McKim, *The Authority and Interpretation of the Bible* (San Francisco: Harper & Row, 1979).

7. John D. Woodbridge, *Biblical Authority* (Grand Rapids: Zondervan, 1982).

We deny that Jesus' teaching about Scripture may be dismissed by appeals to accommodation or to any natural limitation of His humanity.

What this means is that when Jesus speaks in the Gospels about the Old Testament, it is God speaking. What he says is infallible, inerrant, not only in moral and spiritual spheres but also in matters of fact. For example, in Matthew 12:39–41 Jesus speaks of Jonah as though he were a historical person. The Old Testament book of Jonah, therefore, cannot be fiction but must be history.

In Mark 10:4, 5 Jesus accepts the Mosaic authorship of Deuteronomy 24:1–4; in John 5:45–47 he speaks of Moses as author of parts of Scripture; in John 7:19 he says Moses gave the Law. Moses, therefore, must be the author of the Law.

In Matthew 22:43–45 Jesus says that David spoke the words found in Psalm 110:1. David, therefore, must be the author of at least that psalm. In Matthew 23:35 Abel is spoken of by Jesus as a historical figure, and in Luke 17:27 Noah is referred to by Jesus as a historical figure. These references guarantee that at least these two parts of Genesis 1–11 must be historical fact.

The working assumption in this kind of reasoning is: When Jesus speaks, even in the area of matters of fact, it is God the Son speaking.

Jesus' Humanity Is As Essential to Our Salvation As His Divinity

It is not necessary to do more than scratch the surface of this way of looking at Jesus to lay bare its christological assumptions—the assumptions the authors are making about the Person of Christ. These presuppositions are Apollinarian at worst, Monophysite at best. Neither of these ways of thinking is in line with "Chalcedonian orthodoxy" (the historic understanding of Christ which was agreed to in A.D. 451 at the Council of Chalcedon).[8]

8. For what follows, see Bernhard Lohse, *A Short History of Doctrine*, F. E. Stoeffler, trans. (Philadelphia: Fortress, 1966), 82–95. An

The Council of Nicea (A.D. 325) concluded that Christ was fully God and was made human. On the basis of this Nicene orthodoxy, the further question arose as to the relation of the divine and the human in Christ. One approach to the christological problem involved a practical absorption of Christ's humanity into his divinity. This solution is best exemplified by Apollinaris, bishop of Laodicea in Syria (about A.D. 390). Assuming that human beings were composed of body, soul, and mind, Apollinaris said that Jesus had a human body and human soul, but instead of a human mind there was the divine Logos, the second member of the Trinity.

Since Apollinaris' view denied Christ's humanity, it was condemned by Rome in 377 and 382, by Antioch in 378, and finally by the so-called Council of Chalcedon in A.D. 451.

The creed which came from that council spoke of Christ as "in *two natures*, inconfusedly, unchangeably . . . the *distinction of natures being by no means taken away by the union*, but rather the *property of each nature being preserved*, and concurring in one person and one subsistence . . . the Lord Jesus Christ" (italics mine).

This is one of those bedrock Christian beliefs on which Catholics and Protestants agree. John Calvin echoed Chalcedon when he said, "the divinity was so conjoined and united with the humanity, that *the entire properties of each nature remain entire*, and yet the two natures constitute only one Christ" (italics mine).[9]

After the Council of Chalcedon, the opponents of the orthodox view of Christ were the "Monophysites," believers in one nature. They contended that the human in Christ was real, but that it was so subordinated that the ultimate reality was only divine.

Whether Apollinaris before Chalcedon, or the Monophysites afterwards, the position these people held was that Jesus' humanity was swallowed up by his divinity. With Apollinaris the

---

argument similar to my own may be found in R. E. Brown, "'And the Lord Said'? Biblical Reflections of Scripture as the Word of God," *Theological Studies*, 42 (1981): 3–19.

9. John Calvin, *Institutes of the Christian Religion*, II:14:1.

focus was on Jesus' mind, which was not human or subject to human limitations, but rather was the second Person of the Trinity, God the Son. When Jesus spoke, said Apollinaris, even on matters of fact, he transcended human limitations.

Although this error was rejected decisively by Chalcedon (when it spoke of "in two natures . . . the property of each nature being preserved"), this view has reared its head again in these last days in the guise of biblical inerrancy. When inerrantists argue that when Christ speaks even about matters of fact it is God talking, we are to recognize it for what it is, Apollinarian heresy at worst, Monophysite error at best. If Christ's humanity is not to be seen in his being a man of his own times in the area of matters of fact, then I fail to see where his humanity is to be found insofar as his human mind is concerned.

A Confusion That Can Jeopardize the Hope for Eternal Life

It is not difficult to understand why some inerrantists cannot abide the orthodox Chalcedonian affirmation of Jesus' humanity, including the time-conditioned character of his human knowledge in matters of fact. There is in biblical inerrancy a massive confusion about the relationship between finitude and sin—between being finite, and being a sinner. Edward J. Young puts the inerrantists' position succinctly:

> Yet, if Jesus, in his human nature, was subject to fallibility, then, of course, he was not what he claimed to be. He was subject to sin (for *fallibility is the consequence of sin*) and so he cannot be our Savior (italics mine).[10]

I cannot agree. In matters of fact, fallibility is not the result of sin but the natural by-product of human finitude.

10. Edward J. Young, *Thy Word Is Truth* (Grand Rapids: Eerdmans, 1957), 77, 78. The same underlying confusion is implicit in the ICBI's 1982 statement, where Article 2 reads, "We deny that the humble, human form of Scripture entails errancy any more than the humanity of Christ, even in His humiliation, entails sin."

For example, Paul wrote, "I am speaking in human terms, because of your natural limitations" (Rom. 6:19 RSV).

After the New Testament period and up until Augustine of Hippo (A.D. 354–430), there was a widespread tendency in Christianity to identify sin and evil with the ignorance of the finite mind. But that way of thinking comes from Hellenistic culture, not from biblical faith.[11]

Our finitude, moreover, is not something evil, but something good, because it is created by God (Gen. 1:31). It is, however, sin to reject one's finitude and to grasp for divine knowledge (Gen. 3:5, 6).

For Jesus to have been a man of his own time in his knowledge of matters of fact would not have subverted either his divinity or his sinlessness but instead would have guaranteed his full humanity, including finitude, even the finitude of limited knowledge in matters of fact. Only if he were truly human (including finitude), as well as divine and sinless, could he be our Savior.

It is a soteriological necessity to maintain the Chalcedonian confession if we are to believe our own finitude, including our mental limitations, is not rejected by God but will participate in the salvation of the Last Day, the resurrection from the dead.[12] Christological orthodoxy, therefore, argues for a distinction between matters of fact and matters of religion, not only in the Bible as a whole but also in one's understanding of the Jesus of the Gospels.

It is with a sense of assurance, then, that in my dialogue with the Bible, I listen obediently to what it says about relational or soteriological matters, and find in my ongoing experience with God that its wisdom is fully justified.

11. See Reinhold Niebuhr, *The Nature and Destiny of Man* (New York: Charles Scribner's Sons, 1955), I, 167–177.

12. As B. B. Warfield expressed it, "No two natures, no Incarnation; no Incarnation, no Christianity." B. B. Warfield, *The Person and Work of Christ* (Philadelphia: Presbyterian and Reformed, 1950), 211. Warfield did not, however, see the implications of this correct doctrinal confession for his view of biblical authority.

4

Biblical Inerrancy:
A Guide for the Perplexed

FISHER HUMPHREYS

Like any complex social phenomenon, the ongoing debate among Protestant groups in this country over the authority and truthfulness of the Bible can be interpreted in different ways. In the case of the Southern Baptist Convention, where the controversy has been in progress since 1979, one can interpret the phenomenon politically, sociologically, psychologically, even financially.

And the Southern Baptist controversy can be interpreted theologically. From the beginning, fundamental-conservative leaders within that denomination, such as Texas Appeals Court Judge Paul Pressler, have insisted that their sole concern is theological. More precisely, their concern is for the Bible; still more precisely, their concern is for biblical inerrancy.

Throughout the controversy, Baptist and otherwise, biblical inerrancy has been used, understandably, as a blunt instrument. But biblical inerrancy is a doctrine which can be presented in a thoughtful form as well as in a polemical one. My purpose in this chapter is to describe biblical inerrancy in its sophisticated, thoughtful form. To achieve this purpose, I will first present the central claim of inerrancy. Then I will enumerate some of the qualifications which inerrantists make of their claim, and survey some of the ways in which inerrantists defend their position. Finally, I will summarize the underlying concerns of inerrantists, and also the concerns which noninerrantists have about inerrancy.

Here I want to stipulate what I mean by "noninerrantists."

In this chapter I shall use this word to refer to evangelical Christians who hold a high view of the Bible as the uniquely inspired, authoritative Word of God, but who either do not on their own initiative refer to the Bible as inerrant or else actively oppose the idea that the Bible is inerrant. I am not going to comment on people who hold a naturalistic view of the Bible or who deny that it is revelatory in any sense. That view is not a serious option among conservative Protestant groups in general, or Southern Baptists in particular.

My purpose, then, is to describe the theological doctrine known as inerrancy. Some twentieth-century authors who have defended this doctrine are Donald G. Bloesch, James M. Boice, Norman Geisler, Carl F. H. Henry, Harold Lindsell, John W. Montgomery, J. I. Packer, Clark Pinnock, and Francis Schaeffer. The best-known summary of the doctrine is the Chicago Statement adopted by the International Council on Biblical Inerrancy in 1978; an article entitled "Variations on Inerrancy" by David S. Dockery[1] is a useful summary of various views of inerrancy. Twentieth-century authors with a high view of Scripture who have reservations about (or even criticisms of) inerrancy include William J. Abraham, G. C. Berkouwer, F. F. Bruce, Stephen T. Davis, George E. Ladd, Donald McKim, Leon Morris, and Jack Rogers.

Some Southern Baptists have contributed to the discussion. *Baptists and the Bible* by Bush and Nettles is a sophisticated presentation of inerrancy,[2] and *The Doctrine of Biblical Authority* by Dilday,[3] presents a high view of Scripture that does not emphasize inerrancy. When these books were written, the three authors were all at Southwestern Baptist Theological Seminary.

It is helpful to see the intramural discussion among evangelicals in terms of the Southern Baptist controversy, and to

---

1. David S. Dockery, "Variations on Inerrancy," *SBC Today* (May, 1986), pp. 10–11.
2. L. Russ Bush and Tom J. Nettles, *Baptists and the Bible* (Chicago: Moody Press, 1980).
3. Russell H. Dilday, Jr., *The Doctrine of Biblical Authority* (Nashville: Convention Press, 1982).

see the latter in the wider context of the intramural discussion among evangelicals elsewhere. I think it is helpful also to remember that the same discussion took place several decades ago between B. B. Warfield (who defended inerrancy) and James Orr (who defended a high view of Scripture without inerrancy). The two men respected each other's views, and Orr even invited Warfield to contribute some of the materials on the Bible to the *International Standard Bible Encyclopedia;* Orr himself contributed others on the same subject, thus providing evangelical Christians with both perspectives.

Most readers of this chapter will not be interested in my personal view, nor is it my purpose to attempt to convince anyone of it. For those who are interested, I will say simply that I believe that when inerrancy is qualified carefully, I am unable to detect any substantial differences between it and the high view of Scripture offered by many noninerrantists. I regard the Southern Baptist controversy as unnecessary and unfortunate.

We begin by noting the central affirmation of inerrancy.

The Central Affirmation

The central affirmation of inerrancy is that all of the statements found in the Bible are true. The Bible does not include any false statements of its own. (Of course, it may quote false statements made by others, such as, "The fool says in his heart, 'There is no God,'" Ps. 14:1.) This truthfulness is uniform throughout the Bible, and includes historical and scientific statements, for example, as well as religious and theological ones.

Though the word *inerrancy* is negative in form, it represents a positive position. It affirms the truthfulness of every biblical affirmation. What the Bible states to be the case, is in fact the case.

Qualifications of the Affirmation

Sophisticated presentations of inerrancy include not only the affirmation of inerrancy but careful qualifications of it.

The qualifications vary from writer to writer, but the following are representative and would be acceptable to most of the writers listed in the opening paragraphs of this chapter.

1. *No modern text or translation of the Bible is inerrant;* only the original Hebrew and Greek manuscripts of the Bible are—or, more accurately, were—inerrant. Modern texts and responsible translations are very trustworthy, of course; but inerrancy is affirmed only for the autographs, that is, the original manuscripts. These manuscripts, everyone agrees, no longer exist.

This is the most important of the qualifications of inerrancy. It means that the controversy in the SBC does not concern the Bible we have today. It concerns nonexistent ancient manuscripts. Strictly speaking, we probably ought not to speak of the inerrancy of the Bible, since that suggests to most people that we are talking about the Bible as we now have it. Strictly speaking, we should speak of the inerrancy of the original Hebrew and Greek manuscripts of the Bible.

2. *Everything that the biblical writers thought is not inerrant; only what they intentionally taught in Scripture is inerrant.* This is the least understood of the qualifications; it raises many complex questions.

3. *The Bible was written by men.* It did not fall out of heaven from God. God did not literally dictate the words of the Bible to the human writers. Most inerrantists today acknowledge that the method of inspiration is a mystery. Their concern does not center on how God inspired the Bible, but on the result of his inspiration, namely, an inerrant Bible.

4. *The Bible includes progressive revelation.* Later revelation can clarify and supplement earlier revelation, but it cannot correct it, for there are no errors which require correction.

5. *The biblical writers reported things as they appeared to them.* This means that they often used ordinary language rather than, for example, technical scientific language. The language they used was fully embedded in Jewish and early Christian culture. Nevertheless, the writers gave truth, not error, in everything they taught.

6. *The writers of the Bible did not employ only literal language.* They also used poetry, metaphors, images, analogies, and figures of speech. J. I. Packer, a defender of inerrancy, even hints that there may be "symbolic modes of representation in the story of Adam and Eve"[4] though many (probably most) inerrantists would not go that far. But all allow for some figurative language; their concern is only to say that what is pictured figuratively is truth, not error.

7. *The writers of the Bible may use language that is imprecise or inexact.* They may round off numbers or report events out of their chronological sequence. This does not affect the truthfulness of what they teach. "If God allows imprecision on some matters, it is not the task of the contemporary critic to decide a priori that God has failed to communicate truth. God defines truth."[5] "The difference in the number of years the Jews are said to have been in Egypt [see Gen. 15:13, Exod. 12:41] may be the result of one writer starting from a different point than the other or of one giving an exact figure while the other is rounding the number off."[6]

8. *Writers of the New Testament quote the Old Testament freely.* It is not an error if a quotation differs from the Hebrew text.

9. *The Bible is not all didactic or even narrative.* It includes other genres such as songs, prayers, laws, proverbs, apocalypses, and so on. In every genre, what is given is truth, not error.

10. *The Bible includes teachings which do not appear to be inerrant.* Dr. W. A. Criswell calls these "problems." *The Criswell Study Bible* calls them "inadvertences." Bush and Nettles refer to them as "apparent discrepancies, verbal differences, seeming contradictions, and so forth."[7] Some

4. J. I. Packer, *"Fundamentalism" and the Word of God* (London: Inter-Varsity Fellowship, 1965), 99. And see pp. 181, 182 in this book.
5. Bush and Nettles, 421.
6. James Montgomery Boice, *Does Inerrancy Matter?* (Oakland: International Council on Biblical Inerrancy, 1979), 26.
7. Bush and Nettles, 414.

inerrantists urge scholars to attempt to resolve these difficulties, while others, such as Warfield, feel that they may be safely ignored. But all inerrantists agree that they are not to be called "errors."

11. *Finally, some inerrantists do not insist that the word* inerrancy *be used.* Packer feels it is not an ideal term, and Pinnock thinks it can mislead, though both men use it. Bush and Nettles provide a statement of the position which does not employ the term. Paul Pressler has said that he is working for the reality, not the word.

These are some of the qualifications which inerrantists make of their central affirmation. They are important, and they ought to be better known than they are. It is difficult to resist what Clark Pinnock has said to his fellow-inerrantists: "If we keep secret the manner in which we qualify the term, we give the impression to the general public that we hold a more unlimited inerrancy than we do, and for that reason cast dark suspicion upon fellow evangelicals whose actual view of the Bible may be very close to our own, and who differ from us chiefly in their desire to avoid the term inerrancy."[8]

Defense of the Affirmation

Inerrancy is defended in several ways. Some of these will be listed here. It is important to note that not all inerrantists employ all of these defenses; in fact, some explicitly reject some of them. But all of these defenses do get used by one or more sophisticated defenders of inerrancy.

1. *Jesus taught that the Bible is inerrant.* In my judgment, this is the most important of the arguments, for virtually all Christians would want to adopt the same attitude toward the entire Bible which Jesus held toward the Hebrew Scriptures.

2. *The Bible claims to be inerrant.*

3. *Biblical inerrancy is the church's traditional teaching.*

8. Clark Pinnock, "The Inerrancy Debate among the Evangelicals," in *Theology, News and Notes* (Fuller Theological Seminary, Special Issue, 1976), 13.

4. *Inerrancy is defended deductively.* The following syllogism is representative. Major premise: God does not err. Minor premise: The Bible is God's Word. Conclusion: The Bible does not err.

5. *Inerrancy is not often defended inductively,* because of the kinds of difficulties mentioned in the tenth qualification given above. But one piece of inductive argument does appear, namely, that many of the so-called "errors" of the Bible have turned out not to have been errors at all, so we may reasonably expect that others will be resolved in the future.

6. *Inerrantists believe that to surrender inerrancy is to put other doctrines at risk.* This is a domino effect, or a slippery slide effect; only if we are faithful to inerrancy will we be able to be faithful to traditional doctrines such as Trinity, Incarnation, Atonement, and so on. This is true of ourselves, and it is true also of future generations; we must maintain inerrancy so that our successors will not surrender other doctrines.

7. *Inerrantists believe a church that surrenders inerrancy will cease to be committed to missions and evangelism.* This argument has great appeal in the Southern Baptist Convention because that body was formed for purposes of missions and evangelism. This argument, like the previous one, is an appeal to our special interests; that is, these two arguments are *ad hominem.*

8. *Finally, inerrantists argue that inerrancy must be maintained because no one is able to provide criteria for distinguishing truth from error in the Bible.* In the absence of such criteria, failure to affirm inerrancy undermines the credibility of all of the Bible's teachings, implicitly if not intentionally.

A particularly strong form of this argument runs as follows. Noninerrantists cannot provide criteria for distinguishing truth from error in the Bible. But even if they could, they would have surrendered biblical authority, because they would then be submitting the Bible to a nonbiblical standard or norm.

This list is representative of the ways in which inerrancy is defended. Needless to say, appeal is being made to Christian hearts as well as to Christian minds. That seems appropriate in an issue that concerns us as deeply as this one.

Concerns

Now I want to analyze what I believe to be the concerns of inerrantists. What are their deep, underlying concerns? Also, I want to list some concerns felt about inerrancy by Christians who hold a high view of Scripture but hesitate to affirm inerrancy.

It seems to me that inerrantists have four distinct but related concerns.

First, they are concerned to affirm a supernatural view of the Christian faith in general and of the Bible in particular. They are resisting naturalistic views of the Bible.

Second, inerrantists are concerned to affirm that God has revealed himself. It is not the case that men have discovered God; rather, God has made himself known to men. In particular, the Bible is not (or not exclusively) the human reception of revelation; it is (or is also) the divine initiative of revelation.

Third, inerrantists are concerned to affirm that God has revealed cognitive truth. The Bible gives information that is true, not just information that is helpful in life. The Bible's language is propositional, and the Bible's truth is cognitive. The Bible is cognitively true in details as well as in its general message. And it is true in history and science, for example, as well as in theology and religion.

Finally, since the above are true, the Bible is authoritative. It is a normative guide for life for individuals and also for the church. Because it can be trusted to tell the truth, it can also be depended upon to provide needed guidance.

I understand the inerrantists' concerns, therefore, to be for a (1) supernatural (2) revelation of (3) cognitive truth that is therefore (4) authoritative for life.

Now we will look at the concerns of noninerrantists.

1. *The first concern of noninerrantists relates to the qualifications of inerrancy.* What, they ask inerrantists,

remains of your original assertion after you have qualified it so extensively?

The qualifications are frustrating to both groups. Inerrantists feel frustrated because they believe that they have qualified inerrancy so carefully that no Bible-believing Christian ought any longer to resist it. Noninerrantists feel frustrated because they cannot see why they should be asked to accept a view that seems problematic, only to have to qualify it extensively in order to avoid the problems it creates. Why not just bypass the problems and speak of the Bible as God's uniquely inspired, trustworthy Word?

2. *Noninerrantists find inerrancy distracting.* The intense preoccupation with the autographs can distract from the Bible as we now have it. Surely, they argue, the important thing is the Bible as we now have it; no one says it is inerrant, and we all agree that it is trustworthy. Isn't that enough?

One irony of the discussion is that noninerrantists sometimes affirm a higher view of the Bible as we now have it than inerrantists do! For example, one inerrantist has written: "Biblical inerrantists believe: (1) that present translations are inspired and inerrant to the degree that they accurately represent the original manuscripts; and (2) that God has providentially preserved reliable copies of the original manuscripts, so that competent translations of the Hebrew (Old Testament) and Greek (New Testament) manuscripts are to be viewed as virtually the very Word of God."[9] But surely for Christians it is not enough to say that the Bible is "virtually" God's Word! The Bible—as we have it now, both texts and responsible translations—*is* the Word of God, and it *is* inspired. Noninerrantists freely confess that the Bible we now have is the Word of God, and they do not need to add "to the degree that."

The appeal to the autographs also has implications for the arguments used by inerrantists. Here are two of them.

---

9. George Davis, *A Layman's Guide to the SBC Inerrancy Issue* (Dallas: *Southern Baptist Advocate*, no date), 4.

First, it undercuts the two *ad hominem* arguments for inerrancy, the arguments which say that we must have an inerrant Bible if we are to hold on to other doctrines and to practice missions and evangelism. But inerrantists do not say that we have an inerrant Bible; they say only that men *once had* inerrant manuscripts, but now we have a trustworthy (though not fully inerrant) Bible. Cannot both groups agree that commitment to fundamental doctrines and to missions and evangelism is possible with a trustworthy Bible?

Second, the appeal to the autographs undercuts the argument which says that we must hold inerrancy because no one can provide acceptable criteria for distinguishing truth from falsehood in a Bible with even a single error. But inerrantists do not claim that we have an inerrant Bible to interpret; they say that we have a trustworthy (though not fully inerrant) Bible. Therefore, they need criteria for discerning truth in the Bible we now have, just as noninerrantists do.

3. *Noninerrantists feel that inerrancy is too preoccupied with details in the Bible.* Surely what should concern us, they say, is the great message of the Bible, which culminates in the gospel of the crucified and risen Jesus.

Of course, inerrantists respond that they too are concerned with the great message of the Bible. They do not intend to be preoccupied with details. But noninerrantists say that preoccupation with details is entailed by the term "inerrancy" and keeps coming up in all the discussions. They find that unfortunate and distracting.

4. *Some noninerrantists are uneasy with inerrancy's emphasis on cognitive and propositional truths.* They are concerned that attention to this aspect of the Bible may distract from other aspects. The Bible is more than information for minds; it is also formation for our lives. The formative work of the Bible goes on independent of inerrancy, and inerrancy seems to minimize the importance of formation. If this happens, it becomes more important to say the proper thing about the Bible than to be either a hearer or a doer of the Word. Surely something is unbalanced if this happens.

Noninerrantists want talk about propositional truth to be balanced with talk about how the Bible is a life-changing power and food for the souls of men.

5. *Noninerrantists feel that inerrancy fails to do justice to the larger pattern of revelation,* a pattern which is found throughout the Bible. A larger pattern might include factors such as the following: God created a world that reveals him; God acts in history, and especially in Jesus, to reveal himself; people such as Moses and Isaiah have experiences in which God is revealed to them; a community (Israel or the church) remembers these acts and experiences, and tells these stories; these stories (and many other things) are written down; the community collects these texts and canonizes them; these texts are studied, interpreted, taught, and preached; Christ is the criterion by which the texts are to be interpreted; the Spirit guides in all these processes; God uses the Bible—makes it function—to carry out his work; his work is to save and transform people into a community of faithful disciples; the Bible is sufficient for the purpose God has for it and for the way he uses it to make men wise unto salvation.

Some inerrantists would accept all or part of this larger pattern; some actually resist parts of it. But inerrancy itself does not emphasize this pattern, and many noninerrantists feel that it should be emphasized.

6. *Noninerrantists argue that it is more important to obey the Bible's teachings than it is to say proper things about the Bible.* Of course, inerrantists would agree; nevertheless they do severely criticize people who clearly are doers and hearers of the Word, because they have not honored the Word by describing it as inerrant.

7. *Noninerrantists are not persuaded that inerrancy is the traditional view of the church.* Of course, the church has always believed that the Bible is God's Word. But some factors in the inerrancy doctrine are not traditional. The word itself is not (it does not appear in major Baptist confessions, for example), and the appeal to the autographs is recent. On the other hand, some traditional aspects of the church's

understanding of the Bible have been dropped by inerrantists. For example, it was traditional to regard the method of inspiration as dictation.[10] It seems fair to say that inerrancy shares a high view of Scripture with traditional church teachings, but they are not identical.

Noninerrantists also wonder if Jesus emphasized the inerrancy of the Hebrew Scriptures. Certainly he respected the Scriptures as the Spirit-inspired Word of God, and he even referred to tiny marks in the Hebrew text as being fulfilled (see Matt. 5:18). Yet he never appealed to the autographs as inerrantists do, and he said that although the Torah permitted divorce and taking revenge, these actions were not in fact God's will (see Matt. 5:31, 32, 38–42). It is clear that Jesus held a very, very high view of Scripture; but is it the one that inerrantists emphasize, or rather one that does not stress inerrancy?

The same is true about the Bible's claims for itself. Second Timothy 3:16, 17 may be taken as representative: "All Scripture is given by inspiration of God, and is profitable for doctrine, for reproof, for correction, for instruction in righteousness: That the man of God may be perfect, thoroughly furnished unto all good works" (KJV). Here is a high view of Scripture as God-breathed and profitable for the Christian, but it does not emphasize inerrancy.

8. *Another concern of noninerrantists relates to the second qualification, namely, that the Bible writers were inerrant, not in all that they thought, but in what they intentionally, purposefully taught.*

B. B. Warfield puts this in a fairly clear manner: "No objection [to inerrancy] is valid which overlooks the prime question: what was the professed or implied purpose of the writer in making this statement?"[11] But inerrantists are

10. One of the most influential early books defending inerrancy was *Theopneustia* by L. Gaussen (Chicago: Moody Press, no date); Gaussen used "dictation" as a synonym for plenary verbal inspiration and inerrancy.

11. Quoted in Pinnock, "The Inerrancy Debate among the Evangelicals," 12.

sometimes less precise. For example, here are Bush and Nettles: "Full authority resides only in that which Scripture actually teaches intentionally."[12] The earliest proponent of this view known to me was Charles Hodge, who wrote of verbal inspiration: "It asserts that they [the writers of the Bible] were fully inspired as to all that they teach, whether of doctrine or fact. This of course does not imply that the sacred writers were infallible except for the special purpose for which they were employed."[13]

Now the problem with all this is simply that if what is inerrant is the *intended* teaching, and only that, then whose intended teaching is meant? Was it the meaning intended by the human writer? Or the meaning intended by God? The Warfield quotation seems to say that it is the human writer, but the Hodge quotation seems to move from the human writer to God (who employed the writers for his special purpose). Bush and Nettles seem to refer to the intention of Scripture. This is a personification (people, not texts, have intentions), but it makes the issue even more baffling. Would the intended teaching of a text be the plain teaching of an individual statement, for example? Or would its intended meaning be understood only in the larger context of the entire Bible?

Let us suppose for a moment that some inerrantists would say: What is inerrant is the truth God intended to teach through every verse of the Bible, and you can comprehend that meaning only by seeing the teaching in the overall context of the Bible.

If that is the meaning of inerrancy, then it seems to me to be indistinguishable from the high view of Scripture held by noninerrantists.

9. *Noninerrantists feel that inerrantists often erode the belief in the priesthood of believers and the responsibility of*

12. Bush and Nettles, 411.
13. Charles Hodge, *Systematic Theology* (Grand Rapids: Wm. B. Eerdmans Publishing Co., no date), I, 165.

Christians to interpret the Bible for themselves. Of course, sophisticated inerrancy is theoretically committed to an open Bible to be interpreted by all Christians under the guidance of the Spirit. All that is required is that no interpretation conclude that the Bible teaches error; this means that destructive forms of biblical criticism are to be avoided.

But in practice, in spite of these theoretical commitments, discussions of inerrancy often turn on particular interpretations. In Southern Baptist life, for example, the historicity of Adam and Eve has been a major issue. Whenever this happens, noninerrantists understandably hold the inerrancy position accountable for undermining the priesthood of believers.

10. *Finally, noninerrantists are concerned about the divisive results of inerrancy.* In the case of Southern Baptists, it is difficult to see how to answer this concern, since it is so clearly the case that Christian brothers who share a common gospel, a common Baptist heritage, a common commitment to missions and evangelism, and a common high view of Scripture, are in fact being divided precisely over this issue. On the other hand, inerrantists believe that the division is a consequence of defections from inerrancy.

Conclusion

As a result of the present controversy, the Southern Baptist Convention may be set on a course in which it will ultimately find itself committed, not just to a high view of Scripture, but more precisely, to inerrancy. Should this happen, it will not be because inerrantists have persuaded others of their views. It will have been decided politically. That is the way things are done in large ecclesiastical bodies, and I understand that. But this fact of church life does not cancel out the theological issue which many of the new leaders have affirmed to be their chief concern. I have written this chapter because I agree with them that their views deserve to be taken seriously. But I myself am unable to understand how sophisticated, qualified inerrancy, as described in this chapter, differs substantially from noninerrancy.

PART TWO
THE STUDY OF THE BIBLE

5

Biblical Criticism's Role
The Pauline View of Women
As a Case in Point

CHARLES H. TALBERT

What is biblical criticism? Clarity is essential here. Confusion over the meaning of the word "criticism" has sometimes led to misguided opposition to "critical views" of the Bible. In its usual sense, to criticize usually means "to find fault with" or "to attack." Understood in this way, a biblical critic would be seen as one who attacks the Bible.   *V'u*

This is not at all the way in which biblical scholars use the term. They use it in the sense of the Greek word *kritikos*, that is, a literary expert. Understood in this way, a biblical critic is one who employs in the study of the Bible the same methods used in the study of other literary works, like Homer, Virgil, Shakespeare, and Milton.[1]

The goal of the critical scholar is to *discern the meaning* of the writing, not to disparage it. Because of the danger of misunderstanding, the much-used Southern Baptist *Master-Life* program avoids the term "criticism" altogether and instead speaks of the inductive study of the Bible.

What Questions Are Asked, What Methods Used

In order to discern the meaning of a biblical text, answers to certain questions are sought. The five questions which follow are selected from a much longer list.

1. *Is this material to be studied a part of the earliest and best manuscript tradition?*

---

1. John Dillenberger and Claude Welch, *Protestant Christianity* (New York: Charles Scribner's Sons, 1954), 189.

It is necessary to remember that our English translations of the New Testament are made from a Greek New Testament. This Greek New Testament is itself a modern editor's construction made on the basis of ancient handwritten manuscripts which are copies of copies of copies of the original autographs, or first copies, of which we possess none.

These manuscripts often disagree with one another on matters mostly minor but occasionally major. It is important that the oldest and best manuscripts and readings be chosen when constructing a Greek New Testament so that one can, with confidence, feel this is the oldest and best form of the text available for study. The method used to answer this first question is textual criticism.[2] (Textual criticism is often called "lower criticism" to distinguish it from the other critical approaches, all of which together constitute "higher criticism.")

2. *What is the type of liter re being studied?* Is it history, fiction, poetry, parable, letter, or apocalypse?

Each type of literature or genre is interpreted differently. One does not read poetry as one reads a science textbook, just as one does not read a short story as one does history. Knowing the type or "genre" of material with which one is dealing is a prerequisite to discerning its meaning correctly. The method used to answer this question is genre criticism.[3]

3. *Who wrote this, to whom, when, from where, and why?*

If it is possible to answer such questions, the answers will often assist the reader in discovering the meaning of the text. The method used to answer these questions is historical criticism.[4]

4. *How is the material organized?* Does it employ any stylistic devices that are clues to its meaning? Failure to

2. See A. T. Robertson, *An Introduction to the Textual Criticism of the New Testament* (Nashville: Broadman, 1925).

3. This approach is central to Ray Summers's *Worthy Is the Lamb* (Nashville: Broadman, 1951). See chapter 1, "The Nature of Apocalyptic Literature."

4. Questions such as these are the foundation for Frank Stagg's *The Book of Acts* (Nashville: Broadman, 1955); see 19–27.

recognize such clues is an almost certain guarantee of our misunderstanding an ancient text. The method used to answer such questions is rhetorical criticism.[5]

5. *Are there any parallels to the form and/or the content of the writing elsewhere in the Bible?* Are there any parallels in the milieu, or the environment, of the biblical writers? The methods used to answer these last two questions are biblical theology and history of religions research.[6]

Biblical scholars believe that if one has answers to questions such as these, it will be easier to discern the meaning of the biblical text.

Applying the Methods to a Biblical Text: Paul on Women's Role

It is important to see how such a critical (literary) method works in a concrete setting. Let us turn, then, to 1 Corinthians 14:34–36. In the Revised Standard Version this passage reads as follows (leaving off the phrase at the end of verse 33, which probably belongs to the preceding sentence):

> 34. The women should keep silence in the churches. For they are not permitted to speak, but should be subordinate, as even the law says. 35. If there is anything they desire to know, let them ask their husbands at home. For it is shameful for a woman to speak in church. 36. What! Did the word of God originate with you, or are you the only ones it has reached?

1. This material is a part of the oldest and best textual tradition of the New Testament. Textual criticism tells us this.

2. The material appears in a letter. This is the judgment of genre criticism.

3. It is addressed by Paul, who is in Ephesus, to the church in Corinth in the early fifties in order to clarify a series of questions raised for the apostle in an official letter from the

---

5. Consider its use in C. H. Talbert, *Reading Luke* (New York: Crossroad, 1984), 120–126.
6. Talbert, *Reading Luke*, 78–83.

Corinthian church. These are conclusions of historical criticism. (See 1 Cor. 7:1a, "Now concerning the matters about which you wrote." The substance of that phrase is echoed at 7:25; 8:1; 12:1, and in 16:1, 12).

4. The key to a proper reading of the text lies in a recognition of its organization. This is a question studied by rhetorical criticism. The passage employs a stylistic device used elsewhere in the letter, namely, a diatribe style (see, for example, 6:12, 13; 8:1, and 10:23). In the diatribe style, the writer or speaker first quotes his opponent's position, and then responds with his own.

For example, in 6:12 the apostle quotes his Corinthian opponents' libertine assertion, "'All things are lawful for me,'" before he responds with his own qualification, "but not all things are helpful." Since earlier critical scholarship had shown that the diatribe style is present in this particular passage (6:12), modern translations make that fact clear, for example, by adding quotation marks. (See RSV, NIV, NEB, and TEV.)

This stylistic device was widely used in Paul's time and place. He appropriates it for his own, knowing that his readers would be well aware of its use. It is employed in 14:34–36.[7]

Indications the Diatribe Style Is Used

Several facts assist one in recognizing the presence of diatribe here. First, verses 34 and 35 consist of two admonitions, and a basis for each. Admonition one reads: "the women should keep silence in the churches." Basis one reads: "for

7. The Montgomery translation of the New Testament, early in this century, regarded 14:34, 35 as a quote taken from the Corinthian letter to Paul, not Paul's own point of view. For a full discussion in support of this position, see the following: N. M. Flanagan and E. H. Snyder, "Did Paul Put Down Women in 1 Corinthians 14:34–36?" *Biblical Theology Bulletin*, 11 (1981), 10–12; D. W. Odell-Scott, "Let the Women Speak in Church: An Egalitarian Interpretation of 1 Corinthians 14:33b–36," *Biblical Theology Bulletin*, 13 (1983), 90–93; and Talbert, *Reading Corinthians* (New York: Crossroad, 1987), 91–95.

they are not permitted to speak, but should be subordinate, as even the law says." Admonition two reads: "if there is anything they desire to know, let them ask their husbands at home." Basis two reads: "for it is shameful for a woman to speak in church."

Two things stand out about these words. First of all, they reflect the general cultural values of the time, pagan and Jewish. This point is clear from history of religions research, as two pagan and two Jewish examples demonstrate.

In Livy's account of a speech by the consul Cato against the Roman women (34:1–8), Cato asks, "Could you not have asked your husbands the same thing at home?"

Juvenal, in *Satires*, 6, speaks disparagingly of a woman who boldly rushes around the whole city intruding on the councils of men, and talks down leaders in military clothes, in front of her husband.

Philo, *Hypothetica*, 8:7:14, says: "The husband seems competent to transmit knowledge of the laws to his wife."

Josephus, *Against Apion*, 2:201, says: "The woman, says the Law, is in all things inferior to the man. Let her accordingly be submissive . . . that she may be directed, for the authority has been given by God to the man."

Thus, the content of 1 Cor. 14:34, 35 is not distinctively Christian.

The second thing that stands out concerning these verses is that the position taken in these words runs counter to the position taken by Paul elsewhere. (This issue is a concern of biblical theology.)

Galatians 3:27, 28 reads: "For as many of you as were baptized into Christ have put on Christ. There is neither Jew nor Greek, there is neither slave nor free, there is neither male nor female; for you are all one in Christ Jesus" (RSV). This affirms Paul's belief in Christian equality between the sexes in Christ.

1 Corinthians 11:5 reads: ". . . any woman who prays or prophesies . . ." and 11:13 speaks of the manner in which it is proper for ". . . a woman to pray to God. . . . " These

verses imply that Corinthian women prayed and prophesied in church, and that Paul had no problem with the practice so long as their heads were covered.

Since there is no evidence in the text that different women were involved in 1 Cor. 11:2–6 and in 14:34–35 (for example, celibate women in chapter 11, and wives in chapter 14); and since there is no evidence that different parts of the service are referred to (such as, a time of prayer and prophecy in chapter 11, and discussion after the sermon in chapter 14), one is forced to conclude that, if 14:34, 35 states Paul's own view, it contradicts his stance elsewhere.

Furthermore, verse 36 begins with a particle (*e* in Greek) which is translated "What!" in the RSV. The force of that particle indicates that what has come before is rejected or refuted by what follows. In this case, verses 34 and 35 are refuted by the twofold rhetorical query that follows in verse 36, just as the same particle functions at 1 Cor. 11:22, where Paul describes and then sharply rejects the greedy, "me first" way in which some of the Corinthians had been gathering to have a meal together. ("What! Do you not have houses to eat and drink in?")[8]

Moreover, verse 36 is not directed to women exclusively. The second question of verse 36 ("are you the only ones [the word of God] has reached?") uses a masculine plural, *monous* in Greek. This masculine plural can be understood to refer either to multiple male persons or to people in general in a gender-inclusive sense. It cannot address only female persons.

Taken together, these observations yield the point that verse 36 is not the natural conclusion of the argument in the two previous verses. Rather, if verses 34–36 are read together, then verse 36 is a refutation of verses 34 and 35, not a conclusion drawn from them.

This leads naturally to a reading of this passage as an instance of the diatribe: verses 34 and 35 are Corinthian

8. D. W. Odell-Scott, "Let the Women Speak in Church."

assertions, reflecting cultural values like those of pagans and Jews; and verse 36 is Paul's response, rejecting the Corinthian stance about women. Paul's position here would then be in harmony with that taken in Gal. 3:27, 28 and 1 Cor. 11:2–16. Whereas some Corinthians rejected the participation of women in the leadership of worship, Paul responded with horror.

A Second Text on Women's Role

If we are to deal with the question of the role of women fairly, there still remains the problem of 1 Timothy 2:11, 12: "Let a woman learn in silence with all submissiveness. I permit no woman to teach or to have authority over men; she is to keep silent" (RSV).

How this injunction is to be read depends on one's understanding of the historical context of the document. Why were the pastoral epistles (1 and 2 Timothy and Titus) written?

These three little letters reflect a situation where Gnosticism (an early heresy) is infecting the church and making inroads especially among the women. Second Timothy 3:6, 7 reads: "For among them are those who make their way into households and capture weak women, burdened with sins and swayed by various impulses, who will listen to anybody and can never arrive at a knowledge of the truth" (RSV).

As a defense against error, these three pastoral letters appeal to a principle of succession. The true tradition was passed from God to Paul, and from the apostle to Timothy and Titus, and from them to the faithful men who will teach others also (2 Tim. 1:11–14; 2:2). The point is that if the faithful men properly teach the true tradition—obviously the author has in mind the church officials for whom the qualifications are given in 1 Tim. 3:1–7, as in verse 2, "an apt teacher"— then heresy will be defeated.

In such a context, the defense of the tradition would not be committed to those most swayed by heresy (the women). Rather, they would be prohibited from exercising authority and from teaching.

Recognition of the historical context (as it is illuminated by historical criticism) enables us to see that the injunction against women teaching in church is tied to a particular historical situation. The intent is: When women are the source of heresy, they are not to be allowed to teach.

Priscilla's Prominence

Furthermore, 1 Tim. 2:11, 12 needs to be set alongside Acts 18:24–28. Acts 18:26 says Priscilla and Aquila expounded to Apollos the way of God more accurately. Here a woman teaches a male preacher. If one works with the best Greek text, then Priscilla is mentioned first in this verse. In Acts, the dominant figure in a situation is mentioned first. For example, Acts 13:2 speaks of "Barnabas and Saul." But at 13:13, after Paul becomes the dominant figure in the relationship, Acts speaks of "Paul and his company." These considerations indicate that in the case of Aquila and Priscilla, not only was a woman teaching but also that she was the dominant figure, overshadowing her husband.

Of course, in Acts Priscilla represents the true Pauline tradition, not heresy. Where the woman is a representative of the true tradition there is no reluctance to depict her as the teacher of a male preacher. The key both here and in 1 Timothy 2:11, 12 is faithfulness to the true tradition of Paul.[9] What varies is how that faithfulness is to be insured. In one case it is by the exclusion of women from teaching. In the other case it is by their inclusion.

In conclusion, when we compare the thought of 1 Cor. 14:34–36 with what we find in other Pauline texts—which is an effort to answer question 5 in the list given at the beginning of this chapter—we are able to see the consistency of 1 Cor. 14:34–36, properly understood, with the rest of the New Testament. In this concrete example, biblical criticism can be seen as a helping hand to answer certain key questions about the meaning of a particular text for its original audience.

9. C. H. Talbert, *Acts: Knox Preaching Guides* (Atlanta: John Knox, 1984), 81.

What the Bible Means Today

The question of meaning in the Bible can, of course, be split into two parts: what the Bible meant in its original context, and what the Bible means to its current readers. Biblical criticism aims to deal only with the first half of the question of meaning. In this sense, its approach is, for the church, incomplete because it does not pursue the other dimension, what a text means to us in the here and now. That is the task of the preacher, the teacher in the church, and every Bible reader.

At the same time, although biblical criticism is incomplete, it is crucial for the church. This is so because what the Bible means may be more than what it originally meant, but the "more" must be in continuity with what it meant, not in violation of it. For example, it is difficult to see, once the clear meaning of 1 Cor. 14:34–36 is discerned in its first-century context, how anyone today can exclude women from leadership in worship without violating what Scripture meant and means. In this sense, the critical study of the Bible controls one's current/devotional use of it.

The Scholar as Member of Christ's Body

Because this careful study of what the Bible meant requires a knowledge of the biblical languages (Hebrew and Aramaic for the Old Testament, Greek for the New) and of the environment of the Bible (the ancient Near East for the Old, the Hellenistic world for the New), the church relies on scholars in institutions of higher learning (university and seminary) who devote their lives to the task of carrying the major responsibility for this inductive/literary/critical study of the Bible.

Some scholars do pioneer research and writing and shape the disciplines of ancient Near Eastern and early Christian studies. Other scholars take what has been discovered by the pioneers and popularize it for the more general reader, especially within the church. Both serve the church through the exercise of their gifts of teaching (Rom. 12:6, 7, "Having gifts that differ according to the grace given to us, let us use them: . . . he who teaches, in his teaching" RSV).

It is important that the legitimacy of the various gifts be recognized. Paul's words are an encouragement to us at this point.

> For by the grace given to me I bid every one among you not to think of himself more highly than he ought to think, but to think with sober judgment, each according to the measure of faith which God has assigned him. For as in one body we have many members, and all the members do not have the same function, so we, though many, are one body in Christ, and individually members one of another. (Rom. 12:3–5 RSV)

Those who exercise the gift of teaching in the church by devoting their lives to the critical/literary/inductive study of the Bible are an integral part of Christ's body and do not merit rejection.

> There are many parts, yet one body. The eye cannot say to the hand, "I have no need of you," nor again the head to the feet, "I have no need of you." (1 Cor. 12:20, 21 RSV)

Rather, such scholars need to be heard, if for no other reason than to prevent those who are religiously zealous from expressing their devotion to the Lord in ways that run counter to what the Bible meant and means. The matter of women in ministry is a striking case in point.

6

Authority, Criticism, and the Word of God

ROBISON B. JAMES

Inerrantists of the stricter sort, many of whom reject all higher criticism of the Bible, are convinced that their view of Scripture is absolutely essential. For that reason, they are genuinely bothered by the question, "How far can I cooperate with those who do not agree with my view of Scripture?"[1]

But what if inerrantists recognized, as some of their own number have urged them to recognize,[2] that their approach to the Bible has its limitations, just as every other human approach to the Bible has its limitations? In that event, though remaining committed to their view, they would be able to cooperate in genuine fellowship with others. The question, "How far can I cooperate without compromise?" would disappear, or would lose most of its bite.

1. A leading Southern Baptist inerrantist declared at the 1987 Ridgecrest conference that his group was unwilling to stand before Christ in the judgment "and try to explain to the enthroned Christ that in the interest of peace in the convention we supported either by silence or by resources those who say that His word errs." Paige Patterson, "Response," *Proceedings of the Conference on Biblical Inerrancy*, Michael A. Smith, ed., (Nashville: Broadman, 1987), 93.

2. In "Why the Noninerrantists Are Not Listening," Michael Bauman pleads with his fellow inerrantists to stop using six arguments because they are faulty, including "God inspired the Bible; God does not lie; therefore the Bible is without error." As he is no doubt aware, his logic is more sweeping than his language implies. The rejected arguments cover the entire field of proinerrancy arguments, except for an "open-minded, teachable, objective," case by case study "of the factual accuracy of the Scriptural phenomena." He apparently feels inerrancy is a stagnant cause: ". . . it seems more defections occur in their direction than in ours." *Journal of the Evangelical Theological Society*, 29 (September 1986), 317–324.

Toward that much-desired end, I want to show that elements of resistance to biblical authority are built into the strict inerrancy position. *This chapter is designed to show:* that "strict" or "systematic" inerrancy impedes our hearing and heeding the Bible as authority, or as the Word of God (in the prevailing biblical sense of "the Word of God"), and that biblical criticism is irreplaceable today for the full operation of biblical authority, despite the possible danger of critical methods for faith and the insufficiency of these methods *by themselves* for the religious life.

Spontaneous "Inerrancy," or Simple Biblicism

In speaking of "strict or systematic inerrancy," I am distinguishing it from a "spontaneous" kind of confidence in the Bible that eould be described as belief in inerrancy in a broad sense. A good many rank-and-file Christians, if asked whether there are errors in the Bible, will say no. Usually theirs is the "simple biblicism" about which Clark Pinnock has spoken so well.[3]

If simple biblicists use or acknowledge inerrancy language, they appear to do so primarily to express *an attitude of confidence in whatever the Bible has to say.*

It is important to note that the perspective of these rank-and-file Christians is more an *attitude toward* the Bible than anything we would call a formulated *view* of the Bible, to say nothing of calling it a *theory* that governs their use and interpretation of Scripture. Even if they use inerrancy language in saying what they believe about the Bible, they are not systematic inerrantists in the *operative beliefs* according to which they actually use and interpret the Bible, day by day.[4]

3. See this book's Introduction, chapter 1, and also Clark Pinnock, "What Is Biblical Inerrancy?" in *Proceedings,* 75–77. A powerful expression of this "simple biblicism" is the "Pastoral Plea for Peace Among Southern Baptists" signed by 133 pastors and sent to over 30,000. *SBC Today* 5 (May 1987), 1, 16.

4. I give five examples of wholesome ways in which people who say the Bible has no errors show, by the way they interpret the Bible, that their

The reason I call this perspective "spontaneous" is that it has not been formulated in any important way as a reaction against anything. At one time or another, many simple biblicists have probably run into some of the so-called "difficulties" in the Bible—the Bible's apparent inconsistencies with itself and with the conclusions of earth and life sciences, its ethically troubling passages, and its duplicate accounts, for example. But these people have not stayed bogged down with problems of this kind for any length of time. If they have not ignored or dismissed them, they have resolved them on a common-sense basis, ad hoc, as they arose.

The thing they have not done is formulate, in the teeth of a series of these difficulties, some kind of conceptual apparatus with which to subdue the diversities within the Bible.

Strict or Systematic Inerrancy

By contrast, strict biblical inerrancy can be described as "reactive" and "systematic." It is reactive in the sense that it has been formulated in reaction to a string of difficulties of the kind I have recited in the preceding section, especially the diversities and apparent inconsistencies within the Bible.[5] The view is systematic in the sense that it involves a system of ideas that tells the inerrantist in some schematic way how he should understand, and how he must deal with, the difficulties and diversities in the Bible.

---

working beliefs "are enough to give a strict inerrantist fits," in "Baptist Faith and Message Statement: Best Answer," *SBC Today*, 4 (October 1986), 8, 9.

5. This is true on a broad historical scale as well as in the experience of many individuals, as inerrantist historian Mark Noll has pointed out. Though an intuitive confidence in the Bible's truthfulness had been a common property of Christianity all along, *inerrancy as a formulated doctrine*, says Noll, was elaborated in the late nineteenth century; and it came as a "reaction" to the way some Christians were acknowledging numerous "minor errors" in the Bible as they embraced higher criticism. Noll refers primarily to the American scene, of course. Seventeenth-century Protestant scholastics had already worked out a formidable inerrancy doctrine. Mark Noll, "A Brief History of Inerrancy, Mostly in America," in *Proceedings*, 9, 12, 13.

The scheme of ideas that governs the systematic inerrantist is elaborate—it has a good deal of conceptual content to it—even if it is stated in brief form. Harold Lindsell states it rather briefly in this way: ". . . the Bible and every part of it is free from error," he writes. ". . . the Bible is free from errors in matters of fact, science, history, and chronology, as well as in matters having to do with salvation."[6]

A fuller statement of the strict or elaborate inerrancy view is found in the "Chicago Statements" of 1978 and 1982, which were adopted under the sponsorship of the International Council on Biblical Inerrancy, or ICBI (though the 1978 statement could have other implications).[7]

In any case, it is tremendously important to *keep distinct* the simple and the elaborate views, especially within such conservative bodies as the Southern Baptist Convention. It is possible to arouse enormous suspicion and hostility against people who thoroughly agree with the simple biblicism of the rank and file, by saying these people disbelieve the Bible—when the thing they reject or are noncommittal about is the elaborate inerrancy theory!

How Authority and Inerrancy Differ

"But," one might ask, "is it possible really to accept the Bible's authority without believing that the Bible is inerrant?"

It is true that a book, person, or office must have substantial truthfulness, and substantial consistency or coherence, if it is to be our authority. But once that level of truthfulness and coherence is reached—and no one in conservative or

6. Harold Lindsell, *The Battle for the Bible* (Grand Rapids: Zondervan, 1976), 107.

7. In Art. 13, the 1978 statement quietly makes room for simple biblicism, but its overall effect remains otherwise (especially as linked with the 1982 statement) except where this "room for simple biblicism" is brought out and forthrightly stated. Any believer is a "second class citizen" so long as his or her faith is only quietly tolerated. Norman L. Geisler, ed., *Inerrancy* (Grand Rapids: Zondervan, 1979), 497–502, and Earl D. Radmacher and Robert D. Preus, eds., *Hermeneutics, Inerrancy and the Bible* (Grand Rapids: Zondervan, 1984), 889–914.

moderate circles is likely to doubt that about the Bible—then, from that point on, inerrancy and authority go their separate ways, and show that they are quite different things.

For example: When the Philip Morris Company of Richmond, Virginia installs a new cigarette-making machine, a detailed manual comes with it. Suppose it is inerrant. Does the manual's total inerrancy give it authority in the sense in which the Bible has authority as God's Word? Of course not. The manual's authority is irrelevant to anyone but a few technicians and businessmen. Its inerrancy does not extend its authority beyond that circle one bit.

By contrast, the authority of the Bible means that it is anything *but* irrelevant. The authority of Scripture is its rightful claim to be heard, believed, and obeyed by all. The authority of the Bible is its inescapable and irreplaceable *importance,* for all of us, on the most momentous matters of our lives—who we really are, where we are ultimately headed, how we should live, how we stand with the one Supreme Sovereign in the universe, and what he has done and is doing for our redemption.

Inerrancy alone cannot bestow authority upon a book that lacks authority—that is, authority in the Bible's sense—and the lack of inerrancy could not take from the Bible the authority it so manifestly has.

Accepting the Bible—on Certain Conditions

The push for inerrancy then—where does it come from? It does not come from the divine side. It is not necessary for the Bible's authority. It is *a condition that some human beings place on their willingness to accept the Bible as authority.*

If there is any doubt about that, consider the following outcry, the likes of which one frequently hears in religious groups influenced by fundamentalism: "If there is one error in the Bible *at* any point, *on* any point, we cannot trust any of it."

What is that but a condition we impose upon our readiness to accept the Bible as our authority? That is quite a different matter from putting ourselves at the disposal of Scripture *however God may have chosen to give it.* If we seriously embraced the Bible as God's Word, no less, that would have to be *un*conditional. We would have to let the Bible set *its own* terms, rather than our setting the terms. But we don't. We bargain because we want to set the terms. "All right, God," we say, "I'll accept it. But it must satisfy the following conditions. Please listen closely."

We are like Peter who rebuked Jesus and tried to set him straight, when Jesus said his messiahship involved the lowly path of suffering, rejection, and death (Mark 8:31–33). That is to say, we have our own idea of perfection, and are not attuned to the New Testament idea according to which "perfection" has to do with compassionate suffering and lowly weakness (2 Cor. 12:9; Heb. 2:10; 5:9; Matt. 5:48; Luke 6:36). The Bible must be perfect and glorious in *our* sense, or we shall have none of it![8]

Does the Bible View Itself As Inerrant?

But do we impose inerrancy from our side? Isn't inerrancy the Bible's teaching, and the Bible's understanding of itself? Not according to some of the best prepared, brightest and most devoutly believing scholars. Chapter 2 shows that Jesus did not put his authority and example behind strict inerrancy.

British evangelical New Testament scholar James D. G. Dunn carefully examines the four "pillars of the inerrancy stronghold" (2 Tim. 3:16; 2 Pet. 1:20, 21; John 10:35, and Matt. 5:18) and concludes that the inerrantist interpretation of them is "improbable." He then sets forth a massive amount of other evidence in the Bible to show that the Bible not only

---

8. A. A. Hodge and B. B. Warfield spell out the breathtaking view of God and the world which is basic to strict inerrancy in the fourth and fifth paragraphs of their classic essay, ("Inspiration" *Presbyterian Review,* 2 [1881], 227, 228.) This lofty conception of the "divine element which penetrates and glorifies Scripture at every point" (p. 225) is a dazzling intellectual achievement. But it does not rise out of the Bible and its teaching so much as it is imposed upon the Bible. It glorifies Scripture (contrast Jesus' glorification through crucifixion in the Gospel of John) in a way that is *at odds* with the way God gave us the Bible—just as Peter's idea of the Messiah in Mark 8 is at odds with the way God sent his Son among us.

does not set out to teach its inerrancy; it does not *understand* itself that way, either.[9]

And conservative evangelical Clark Pinnock, after years of struggling with the biblical evidence, wrote: "In the last analysis the inerrancy theory is a logical deduction not well supported exegetically [by the interpretation of biblical passages]. Those who press it hard are elevating reason over Scripture at that point."[10]

Some inerrantists will not be convinced. Does that leave us at an impasse?

It does not. The following conclusion follows without further ado: Strict inerrantists not only *can* accept noninerrantists as equally faithful to Scripture. They must. *The Bible's own authority requires them to do so.*

How so? If they want to rule someone out of court because he or she is not a strict inerrantist, they clearly cannot do it on the basis of the Bible's authority. They have to step outside the Bible and bring in one disputed interpretation *of* the Bible. That is to say, they are forced to *abandon the Bible's authority*, and bring in the authority of this or that creed-like interpretation of it.

Relational or Descriptive?

Our reverent beliefs regarding the Bible function in two ways. Our belief in the Bible may *relate us to* the Bible as our authority—ready to hear it and heed what it has to say. That is relational belief. Or our beliefs about the Bible may *describe and characterize* the Bible as a special kind of book. That is descriptive belief. We can see the two are different because we might believe extraordinary things *about* the kind of book the Bible is, and still not believe it in the sense of hearing and heeding it.

Simple, spontaneous biblicism—our attitude of readiness to hear, believe, and heed what the Bible has to say—

9. James D. G. Dunn, "The Authority of Scripture According to Scripture," *Churchman: A Journal of Anglican Theology*, 96 (1982), 107–113, 118.

10. *The Scripture Principle* (San Francisco: Harper & Row, 1984), 58.

obviously functions primarily so as to *relate* us to the Bible, in a posture of readiness to hear it and heed it. Systematic inerrancy is different. Although it also serves this relational function, it goes beyond that in a decisive way. It also *describes* the Bible, and tells us how to handle what we find in it. This makes it possible for systematic inerrancy beliefs to subvert or short-circuit the Bible's authority over us. An analogy will show how this happens.

A Person As Authority: An Analogy

Just as we wish to accept the Bible as our authority, let us imagine that we want to accept a certain person as our authority. At the outset, we shall imagine that this person is Socrates. Later we will drop him from the analogy.

We commence by noting the difference between these two things: (1) we *commit ourselves* to follow Socrates, to obey him and be faithful to him, and (2) we *describe* Socrates, or *characterize* him in some way.

If we are sincere, our first or relational commitment poses no threat whatsoever to Socrates' exercise of authority over us. On the other hand, when we describe or characterize Socrates, our characterization runs the potential risk of short-circuiting his authority over us.

Why? Because we may hold some beliefs that *mis*describe him in a serious way. If we do, and if we are not quickly dislodged from our faulty characterization of him, then—to the extent that we have misdescribed Socrates—we have made it impossible for him to exercise his authority over us.

For example, we may have thought Socrates—or any person now—was extremely concerned that we be very precise on all details, whereas the person we are trying to accept as our authority is *in fact* a "laid-back" individual, someone who is concerned with the "big picture," someone who would rather we deal with approximations and let smaller things slide, rather than be hasty with people, or compulsive with details.

Perhaps this person is like Jesus with Mary as contrasted with Martha, or like Jesus with the Prodigal Son as contrasted with the Elder Brother, or like Jesus with the tax

collectors and prostitutes who would enter the kingdom before the Jewish religious leaders of his day (Luke 10:38–41;
15:20–32; Matt. 21:31). In any case, if our description of the
person we want to accept as our authority varies from what
this person is really like, then even though we intend to be
faithful and obedient to him, we will interpret each signal
from him in one way, whereas he will have meant many of
those signals in another way.

The difference between what this person really intends
and what we think he means may be small in some cases. But
the difference may be quite large in other cases. *Unfortu-
nately, the differences can be very large indeed where it is a
question of the person's basic perspective upon life.*

When that happens, this person's authority over us is short-
circuited in a devastating way. Like Luther or Saul of Tarsus,
we may do a prodigious number of things this person tells us
to do. We may quote him all the time. But at the key points
we do all this for the wrong *reasons.* We get a lot of the words
right. But we never get the music.

Thus we are taking a risk when our beliefs describe the
Bible. If our descriptive beliefs about the Bible are off, we
may very well be subverting the Bible's authority over us.

Pharisaic Bible, Legalistic God

James D. G. Dunn finds that the kind of inerrancy doctrine
found in the ICBI's Chicago Statement runs a grave risk
of Pharisaic legalism. He demonstrates the point rather con-
clusively by observing certain characteristic moves which
ICBI-type inerrantists make, such as their "harmonizing
expedients."[11] Dunn is correct. But his point is actually
stronger than he has stated it. The strict inerrantist has already committed himself to a legalistic God and a Pharisaic
Bible—without intending to do so, of course—even before he
starts interpreting any Bible passages.

When strict inerrancy assumes that God is the kind of

11. J. D. G. Dunn, "The Authority of Scripture," 116, 117.

Speaker who wills with some intensity that absolutely every word in the Bible, no matter how peripheral to the Bible's main purposes and no matter how many problems it may seem to raise, shall stand as "inerrant" in the strict inerrantists' sense, inerrancy therewith assumes something about the character of God himself (without intending to). It assumes *in* God, and attributes *to* God, a legalistic mindset and a meticulous, hyperscrupulous nature that is simply inconsistent with some of the most distinctive emphases of Jesus,[12] Paul,[13] the prophets,[14] and others.

I am not saying that we only need to consider the image of God we get from Jesus' parable of the Prodigal, from his attitude toward Martha, and from his taking up for tax collectors and prostitutes. Nor am I saying that the one and only theme from Paul we should listen to is "the letter kills, but the Spirit gives life" (2 Cor. 3:6). But I am saying this: These things are very, very central. And there are a lot more things in the Bible of the same stripe. But note: The issue here is *not* that we want to pick and choose what to believe. Rather, we are asking what happens when we yield ourselves fully to Scripture *without preconceptions.* When we do, Scripture itself imposes some of its claims upon us as *priority, overriding claims.* This should not be surprising. Jesus was famous (and got killed) for saying that some claims were "priority" or "overriding" in this way.[15]

Thus, if the Bible is to be our authority on the character of God, we cannot sweep these things under a rug. We must not "stack the deck" by committing ourselves, ahead of time, to some description of God that ignores or stifles these startling, life-giving, evangelical themes. (I use "evangelical" in the sense of "evangel," the "gospel" or "*good* news.")

12. In addition to the themes I have noted in the text above, see chapter 2.
13. 2 Cor. 3:6, 12–17; Rom. 7:6.
14. Micah 6:6–8 (cited by Jesus, Matt. 23:23); Jer. 31:31–34.
15. See Mark 3:6 as the conclusion of 2:1–3:6. Cf. also the "It was said . . . but I say . . ." pattern in Matt. 5:21–48; and the readiness with which Jesus promoted two commandments above the others, Mark 12:28–34; and Mark 1:22; 2:27. And see chapter 2.

Yet that is precisely what a strict inerrancy view does. It "stacks the deck" in the way I have described. Of course it does not mean to do that. A systematic inerrantist will insist that his inerrancy method will *keep* him from overlooking the Jesus-Paul-prophets sorts of things I have noted. He will be absolutely sure his inerrancy method will force him to give due emphasis to those liberating evangelical themes, along with everything else in the Bible.

But it won't happen. Not if the strict inerrantist sticks by his principles. Once he gives every single fragment of Scripture the status, in effect, of a piece of the puzzle that has got to stand tall and fit snugly into the big picture somehow, here is the result: the Jesus-Paul-prophets themes, which are so central and decisive in both testaments, lose all hope that their *obvious priority status* can be respected.[16] In that way the authentic biblical image of God is skewed beyond redress by the first, unrevisable, logically controlling step strict inerrancy takes.

Staying Correctable

How shall we avoid misdescribing the Bible and misdescribing God in this way? Should we make sure our belief in Scripture does nothing but "relate" us to the Bible? Should

16. Theoretically speaking, the Chicago statements may not rule out all possibility of priority, overriding claims in the Bible. But there is a strong tendency in the direction of "leveling" everything. The way the statements deal with one passage correcting another (at least in the 1982 statement, as in Art. 17) is so rigid that adherents of these statements have a tough time yielding to the Bible's authority when they run up against a truly priority claim. (And who are we to tell God he cannot put overriding claims in the Bible?) In theory, Chicago adherents may manage to admit that a claim has priority. But in their attitudes and ongoing lives it is virtually impossible. At least at the back of their minds they know that they (or someone) must *harmonize this priority claim somehow* with other things in the Bible that do not fit together with it very well. So they chip away at the specialness of the claim—a priority claim!—scaling it down to fit some things it probably is supposed to override. The rigid complexities of the Chicago statements are a bit like Saul's armor which the boy David put on—only to find he could not walk! (1 Sam. 17:39).

we purge our beliefs of everything that would "describe" Scripture one way or another?

No, that is not possible. And it is not desirable, anyway. It is inevitable that our beliefs about the Bible will characterize the Bible in some way. And, within limits, it is perfectly healthy that they should. Faith has no "that" without a "what." The fact "that" we believe in the Bible always involves some notion of "what" sort of book we believe in. We describe anything we relate to, in the very process of relating to it.

But there is one thing we can do. We can keep our descriptive beliefs from becoming so hard, so fixed, and so controlling that *we take those beliefs more seriously than we take what confronts us in the Bible itself.* We can keep our descriptive beliefs about the Bible subject to revision by what we learn, as we continue to *relate* ourselves directly to the Bible itself.

But that is precisely what strict inerrancy cannot do and will not do (except when it forgets its own principles). On its basic descriptions of the Bible strict inerrancy refuses to budge or bend in any way, no matter *what* it finds in the Bible, no matter *how* God gave it, and no matter *in what way* God desires to speak to us through it. Come what may, the Bible must be conformed to the inerrancy theory, not the other way around. Strict, systematic inerrancy is *designed* to be uncorrectable by anything it might find in the Bible.

That is why strict, systematic inerrancy makes it more or less impossible for its adherents to fully—and I mean fully—relate themselves to the *Bible* as their actual authority. Such inerrancy really wants its disciples to relate only to the Bible *as the Bible has first been conformed to their theory of it.* The minute one of these disciples gets out of line and appeals directly to what he finds in the Bible, he feels the heat.[17]

17. Robert Gundry's eviction from the Evangelical Theological Society is a case in point. Cf. Leslie R. Keylock, "Evangelical Scholars Remove Gundry for His Views on Matthew," *Christianity Today,* 28 (February 3, 1984), 36–38.

The lesson here is that we must keep our *descriptive* beliefs about the Bible on a tight leash. We must keep them under the control of our *relational* belief in the Bible. Our descriptions must be correctable. Otherwise they become a threat to the Bible's authority over us.

Two Ways to Believe the Bible Is God's Word

If we believe the Bible is the Word of God with a *relational* kind of belief, that means: We relate ourselves to the Bible as our authority because we receive it as *God addressing us*. It is "His Word" in that very relational sense. Interestingly, this was Martin Luther's attitude toward the Bible.[18]

On the other hand, if we believe the Bible is God's Word with a *descriptive* kind of belief, that means: We agree to certain descriptions of the Bible, how it was produced (by inspiration), and what kind of book resulted (a record of God's words). That is the main thing strict inerrancy does. It characterizes the Bible according to a picture which, briefly sketched, looks like this: Centuries ago, God worked in the lives and minds of certain authors so that they wrote, not precisely the Bible we have, but the "autographs" of these sixty-six books. And God saw to it that no mistakes were made back then.

It is important to note the "back then" emphasis of this view. The picture the inerrantist draws is actually clearer if God is *absent* here and now, today. The usual inerrantist picture gets blurred the minute we try to reckon with "God here and now speaking." The effort threatens to blow a fuse, so to speak.

Of course, inerrantists' overall beliefs do not require God to be absent today. But their typical *doctrine of Scripture as the Word of God* usually leaves him out of the here and now. It says nothing about "God here and now speaking." Their

18. David Lotz, "*Sola Scriptura:* Luther on Biblical Authority," *Interpretation*, 35 (1981), 271.

belief that the Bible is God's Word is mainly, if not entirely, a "back then" kind of thing.[19]

By contrast, when I believe the Bible is God's Word in a relational way, I am putting myself on the line that God is really *there*, that His Spirit is *present*, and that God himself *addresses* me (see 2 Cor. 3:16, 17).

Which of these two ways of believing the Bible to be the Word of God is more biblical? There is not the slightest doubt. The first, or relational kind of belief is found at the center of what the Bible is talking about when it speaks, hundreds of times, of "the Word of God," "the Word of the Lord," "the Word," etc.[20]

On the other hand, the descriptive kinds of belief regarding "the Bible as God's Word" are taught in only a couple of New Testament passages, and implied in not a great many others.[21]

I used to worry about that. I was not prepared to quit calling the Bible "God's Word." But I asked myself whether that way of speaking was a tradition that obscured something important the Bible was trying to say. Was it *biblical* to talk like that, I asked myself, when "the expression 'Word of God' in Scripture *does not usually refer to the written word at all*, but rather to God's or his emissaries' speaking and inspiration"?[22]

19. From the 1978 Chicago Statement, Art. 10: ". . . copies and translations of Scripture are the Word of God to the extent that they faithfully represent the original." N. L. Geisler, ed., *Inerrancy*, 496. The same point is made in a typical popular presentation of strict inerrancy, James Draper, *Authority* (Old Tappan, N.J.: Revell, 1984), 82.

20. Cf. John Reumann, "The New Testament Concept of the Word," *Consensus: A Canadian Lutheran Journal of Theology*, 4 (July 1978), 15–24; and 5 (January 1979), 15–22.

21. 2 Tim. 3:16; 2 Pet. 1:20, 21.

22. *Harper's Bible Dictionary*, Paul J. Achtemeier, ed. (San Francisco: Harper & Row, 1985), 1141, under "word," emphasis added. Many Christians are not aware of this fact, even though it has large implications for the way we understand the Bible. In an address at the 1987 Ridgecrest conference, SBC President Adrian Rogers quoted some fifteen new Testament passages which refer to "the Word of God" and said they were

Then it struck me. We can say the Bible is the Word of God, and say it primarily in the Bible's own prevailing sense—in the relational sense I have been talking about. The Bible is God's Word in the sense of his living address to us. This does not require us to abandon the descriptive or "back then" kind of belief that the Bible is God's Word. But it does tell us to keep it where the Bible keeps it, namely, in a position that is secondary to the "relational" sense.

If we keep the descriptive subordinate to the relational in this biblical way, that will get us out of the business of telling God ahead of time how he must speak, or did speak, in the Bible. For example, if God wishes to give some of the evangelical notes in Scripture a *central, priority, overriding* status, we will not be busily setting him straight by propping up the things the Bible itself tells us to keep peripheral.

Criticism: Ally of Biblical Authority

In the preceding chapter, Charles Talbert has done a beautiful job explaining most of the "critical" approaches to the Bible, and showing how essential they are if we are to get at what the Bible means.[23] Even if one disagreed with Professor Talbert's conclusion about the Pauline view of women, the only way to answer him would be to deal with his evidence,

---

speaking of the Bible (*Proceedings*, 125–127). At a news conference the next day, two of the featured inerrantist experts at Ridgecrest (Clark Pinnock and Kenneth Kantzer) pointed out that in all but one of Rogers' cases, or in all but a few, "the Word of God" means the gospel message, *not* the Bible (audiotape in the editor's files).

23. Because Talbert dealt mainly with a letter in the New Testament, he had no occasion to discuss three approaches used for primarily *narrative* parts of the Bible, such as the Gospels. *Form criticism* asks about the "oral stage" of the tradition about Jesus—the sorts of oral accounts Paul tells us he received from others *before the gospels were written* (1 Cor. 7:10, 11:23, 15:3). A conclusion of *source criticism* is that both Matthew and Luke drew upon Mark as a source, plus another source which no longer exists ("Q"). *Redaction criticism* examines the way a biblical writer edited his materials together, or "redacted" them, into a unified whole. It asks, what is Matthew's unique viewpoint and theology (or Mark's, or John's, etc.)?

that is, to use one or more of the critical approaches he has employed.

What this means is clear: biblical authority mandates the use of critical approaches. If we hamstring critical scholarship on the Bible with preconceived or purely traditional ideas, we ipso facto encroach upon the authority of Holy Scripture. It is simply fraudulent to say the Bible is our authority—if we are simultaneously taking steps to shield ourselves from the most objective information we can get about the Bible and what it means.

Of course, critical study of the Bible can be presented in a way that tends to disrupt faith. Ordinary Christians need the coaching of godly, scholarly pastors and teachers to help them understand the methods, and appropriate the new insights derived from those methods. But it is a mistake to say the *critical methods themselves* are a threat to biblical authority. They are irreplaceable today for the full operation of biblical authority.

One of the most mischievous misconceptions visited upon the church in the last century is the idea that biblical inerrancy is an *infallible ally* of biblical authority, while criticism is its *natural enemy*. In decisive respects, the opposite is the truth.

Criticism is an ally of biblical authority, provided the scholars doing the critical study are able to keep their inquiries from being dominated by their ideological biases (especially any naturalistic biases). The scholarly community, operating *over time* as an interacting whole, approximates that ideal to a considerable degree. And the scholarly community would do a far better job if more evangelical scholars were doing their part—rather than arguing about inerrancy.[24]

24. "Tony Thiselton once told me," Clark Pinnock said, "that he did not pay much attention to the debates over biblical inerrancy because he wanted to make progress in his studies of biblical and philosophical hermeneutics. I'm glad that he did. Inerrancy theory can be very distracting if you take it seriously." Clark Pinnock, "Parameters of Biblical Inerrancy," in Michael A. Smith, ed., *Proceedings*, 98.

That is not a flippant remark. I believe God is calling scholarly pastors and teachers in this day to a most demanding task. It is the task of working out for future generations something that previous generations simply have not had: the rudiments of a nourishing, evangelical employment of the proven, critical approaches to the Bible.

The time is ripe. I try to explain why the time is ripe in the introduction to the next chapter. There is a fluidity and even a humility in much of the scholarly world that has not often been there. And Southern Baptist pastors and teachers are almost uniquely positioned to seize these "new openings for biblical authority."[25]

But as surely as God calls to a great work, tragedy impends. The largest body of Baptists on earth seems on the verge of deciding that *only non-Baptists* can teach or lead in their denomination—neutered individuals devoid of the Baptist soul-freedom to submit directly *to the Bible*, as authority, rather than to someone's *theory about* the Bible.[26] And make no mistake. It will be a tragedy of historic proportions if the pastors and teachers who are equipped to do this work are hounded into exile, or threatened into silence.

25. Cf. Marvin E. Tate, "New Openings for Authority," *SBC Today* 4 (March 1987), 6–8.

26. The "Pastoral Plea for Peace" (footnote 3 in this chapter) speaks pointedly: "The right and burden of private interpretation is as binding upon teachers, preachers, and employees of the denomination as it is upon anyone else. One does not forego or escape this right and duty by accepting denominational employment, any more than the preacher is bound to speak from the pulpit only the thoughts of the people who pay him." *SBC Today* 5 (May 1987), 16.

PART THREE
THE AUTHORITY OF THE BIBLE
Views Which Shape Belief Today

7

A. T. Robertson: The Evangelical Middle Is Biblical "High Ground"

EDGAR V. MCKNIGHT

Editor's Introduction

When Edgar McKnight speaks of the "high ground" occupied by A. T. Robertson, he has in mind the way the great New Testament scholar pursued his vast learning *in the service of preaching*. This fact about Robertson (1863–1934) makes him surprisingly contemporary.

Recent Changes Prefigured

In an interesting way, Robertson's combination of scholarship and piety prefigures a major shift which has been going on since the late 1960s among front-rank Bible scholars, a shift beautifully described for laypeople by Marvin Tate in the March 1987 *SBC Today*.[1] One important change has been the realization by these scholars that the historical-critical method (as they had been practicing it) was not achieving its intended purpose. It was not interpreting Scripture so "that the past becomes alive and illumines our present with new possibilities. . . ."[2]

This development should not be misunderstood. Most Bible scholars have been devout church people all along. They never ceased to use the Bible in their preaching and their devotional life. But their historical-critical studies did not always support their piety, or mix well with it.

These scholars have not abandoned historical criticism. Nor have they turned their backs on the enormous and ever-

---

1. Marvin E. Tate, "New Openings for Authority" (in the "Confronting the Bible" series), *SBC Today* 4 (March, 1987), 6–8.
2. Walter Wink, *The Bible in Human Transformation* (Philadelphia: Fortress Press, 1973), 2.

accumulating knowledge that method yields. What they have done is to *reshape* the method, especially by supplementing it with newer approaches. Using the newer approaches, they are no longer content simply to pin down the historical origins of biblical texts, or identify the sources the author used, or explain how the texts reached their final form. And they are not satisfied merely to reconstruct the history which lies "behind" the texts.

Rather, standing "in front of" the texts, many of these individuals make it part of their scholarship to confront the Bible as a book that speaks from faith to faith. For example, in Genesis 3, the yearning, loss of innocence, and sense of estrangement from God become the subject for treatment—rather than the similarities of the story to what might be found in other literatures. In that way the gap between scholarship and devout listening is closed. In Tate's fine phrase, the fresh approaches to Scripture repeatedly provide "new openings for biblical authority."

"Our Historic Tradition": How Important Is That Question?

McKnight's chapter has some telling implications for the debate raging within this country's largest Protestant denomination. One of the questions in dispute is this: "What is the historic view of Southern Baptists concerning the Bible?"

There is a prior question, however. We can also ask: "How important is this whole issue in the first place?" The answer—though we would hardly guess it listening to Southern Baptists argue—is that the question *cannot be decisive for Baptists,* or certainly not in the way it can be for some other religious groups. As one of the Southern Baptist fundamental-conservatives expressed it, "Baptists . . . are not bound by their tradition. . . ." That is the judgment of Richard Land of Criswell College.[3]

Actually, Baptists are not altogether unique in making this point, at least among Protestants. They simply put more stress on it than many others do. For Baptists it is a matter of principle that they should *not* be bound by their tradition (cf. Mark 7:13).

---

3. Land qualified the statement appropriately, but he made it with conviction. Richard D. Land, "Response," in *Proceedings of the Conference on Biblical Inerrancy 1987* (Nashville: Broadman, 1987), Michael A. Smith, ed., 32.

Nothing in their past is to assume the authority over them which belongs to the Bible alone.

This emphasis takes on special importance where a traditional view of the Bible is concerned. Even if some of the most important figures in the Baptist past held this or that view of the Bible, Baptists of today would be *obligated* to differ with them—if the Bible itself so required.

The Princeton View Not "Foundational"

Granted that "the historic tradition" cannot be decisive, the issue is still of considerable interest. One of the key questions can be stated in this fashion: Which view is standard-setting or normative among Southern Baptists, (1) the "simple biblicism" discussed in chapter 1, or (2) a "strict," "elaborate" inerrancy view, especially the doctrine of the Princeton Seminary Presbyterians, Charles Hodge, A. A. Hodge, and B. B. Warfield?

Some vocal Southern Baptist fundamental-conservatives (including at least two who spoke at the 1987 Ridgecrest conference) are convinced that the Princeton view is "foundational" in the denomination's seminary education, or in its organized convention life. They base that opinion on their belief that the original faculty at Southern Seminary held a Princeton view.[4]

They are correct about two of these founding fathers, J. P. Boyce and Basil Manly, Jr. Both had studied at Princeton, notably under Charles Hodge. However, McKnight's evidence shows that the third key member of that first faculty, New Testament and homiletics professor John A. Broadus, did not hold a Princeton view. For one thing, he distanced himself from the idea that the Bible is verbally inspired.[5]

---

4. L. Russ Bush, "The Roots of Conservative Perspectives on Inerrancy (Warfield)" in Michael A. Smith, ed., *Proceedings*, 281; and Richard Land, "Response," 35.

5. Does an 1892 catechism under Broadus' authorship indicate that he held a Princeton view? The document, published for youths of ten to fifteen years, certainly sounds inerrantist in some sense. Relevant parts are quoted in L. Russ Bush and Tom J. Nettles, *Baptists and the Bible* (Chicago: Moody Press, 1980), 225, 226. The catechism cannot offset the evidence McKnight supplies, however. Thus James Draper is not justified in concluding from it that "Broadus was an inerrantist in the fullest sense of the word," or in using Broadus as evidence that "Baptists' historical position" is the Princeton view. See Draper's *Authority* (Old Tappan, N. J.: Revell, 1984), 62, 54.

And we may add a fascinating piece of evidence that McKnight does not mention. The seminary founders drew up a confessional statement in 1858, the Abstract of Principles. Faculty at the school still sign it. If the founders had believed the Princeton view was "foundational," they would surely have written it into that Abstract, at least in an early, pre-Warfield version. But they did not do so.

In fact, they made a daring change in precisely the opposite direction. The basis for their statement on the Bible was the Philadelphia Confession of 1742, which is identical at this point and at most points with the Second London Confession of 1677 and 1688. The opening words of these confessions are:

> The Holy Scripture is the only sufficient, certain, and *infallible* rule of all saving Knowledge, Faith, and Obedience.[6]

The seminary founders deleted the word "infallible," despite its well-known history, and inserted the word "authoritative" instead.[7] They could not make such a change "under a bushel," and they knew it. But they made it anyway. Thus the Abstract opens:

> The Scriptures of the Old and New Testaments were given by inspiration of God, and are the only sufficient, certain and *authoritative* rule of all saving knowledge, faith and obedience.[8]

---

6. William L. Lumpkin, *Baptist Confessions of Faith* (Philadelphia: Judson Press, 1959), 248, emphasis added.

7. Even in its original wording, this Baptist affirmation says, not that the Bible is infallible, but that it is an infallible rule—on salvation matters.

8. Robert A. Baker, *A Baptist Source Book* (Nashville: Broadman Press, 1966), 138, emphasis added. Richard Land thinks Manly interprets this sentence in Princeton terms in an 1882 letter where Manly says this sentence means "the Scriptures are so inspired as to *possess* infallibility and divine authority . . ." (Land, "Response," 36, emphasis added). But Manly, speaking for Broadus as well as for himself and Boyce, has chosen his words carefully. To say the Bible "possesses" infallibility is not the same as saying it is infallible on any question we might be curious about. The infallibility the Bible "possesses" might pertain, for example, to its substance. Broadus made a distinction between "truth in substance" and "truth in statement," as McKnight shows.

Robertson Was a "Simple," Not An "Elaborate," Biblicist

McKnight's essay also puts to rest a claim often made or implied, to the effect that the Princeton tradition was carried into the twentieth century by A. T. Robertson, who was probably Southern Baptists' most influential biblical scholar.

At the 1987 Ridgecrest conference, Richard Land held aloft a photocopy of an 1892 speech by Robertson, and quoted from it in ringing terms to drive home the point that Robertson took the Princeton view. True enough, Robertson took that view in that speech. But Land's presentation created the impression, which is apparently his belief, that the 1892 speech is definitive regarding Robertson's position.[9]

But it is not. Even when Robertson delivered the speech he made some apologetic remarks about it, as McKnight reports. And, more important, Robertson wrote the speech while still under Manly's influence, three years *before* he moved fully into his chosen field of New Testament. McKnight describes the change by which Robertson came to his mature view in the following way. "In direct confrontation with the biblical text and released from the need to provide a rationale for a given view of inspiration and authority, Robertson moderated his position."

What kind of change is this? It looks for all the world like a great scholar's return from an "elaborate" Princeton view to the "simple biblicism" of his Baptist heritage. In that respect—and also in his capacity to adapt to new methods of critical study— Robertson is a worthy model for us today. But not as a protagonist of the Princeton view. For he had abandoned that view by 1895, or by very few years thereafter.

---

9. Reporting on the Ridgecrest conference, the *Southern Baptist Advocate* (June, 1987, 8, 9) declared that Land's presentation delivered "devastating blows" to the idea that inerrancy lacked "historicity in Baptist life," and quoted Robertson's 1892 speech at length. The paper is the organ of politically mobilized fundamental-conservatives, and is sent free to some 65,000 people (cf. its April 1987 issue, p. 1). Cf. Land, "Response," 37, 38. Land comments, "If you read his subsequent work, certainly Robertson did not [change]," 44, note 52.

Archibald Thomas Robertson, who taught at Southern Baptist Theological Seminary for almost forty-six years (1888–1934), is usually conceded to be the greatest Southern Baptist scholar of the first half of this century. Professor of New Testament Interpretation from 1895 until his death, this author of nearly fifty books and one thousand articles left a stamp upon Southern Baptists second to none, certainly insofar as the use of the New Testament is concerned. Nor was his influence limited to Baptists.

During much of Robertson's career, Protestants in this country were being polarized into warring camps. The middle ground—the high ground from which the biblical Word is *experienced and preached* rather than *fought over*—was being eaten away.

Spared much of this turmoil, Southern Baptists were able to retain a great deal of that middle ground. They continued to maintain confidence in the trustworthiness of the Bible while benefiting from some of the newer developments in biblical study. Nowhere was this done more tellingly than in the life's work of A. T. Robertson.

Robertson's evangelical conservatism is undisputed. It is heralded by Southern Baptist inerrantists[1] and by far-right fundamentalists.[2] But it is not as widely recognized that his position (with the possible exception of a few years around 1890) was an "evangelical middle" which avoided not only liberalism on the left, but also the fundamentalist view of biblical inerrancy on the right.

The 1880s and 1890s at Southern Seminary

Robertson came to Southern Baptist Seminary as a student in 1885. During the closing decades of that century, Southern

1. L. Russ Bush and Tom J. Nettles, *Baptists and the Bible* (Chicago: Moody Press, 1980), 286, 300–303.
2. David O. Beale, *S. B. C.: House on the Sand?* (Greenville, S. C.: Unusual Publications, 1985), 29, 30, 121.

Baptist leaders assured Baptists of the trustworthiness of the Bible by using language which at times was akin to earlier pietistic experiences, while at other times it was similar to the fully developed doctrine of biblical inerrancy formulated during that period by the Princeton Presbyterians, A. A. Hodge and B. B. Warfield.

An example of the simpler, more pietistic way of speaking can be found in John A. Broadus, one of the four original professors at Southern Baptist Seminary. In a sermon before the Southern Baptist Convention in 1883, he declared that it was not wise to formulate a theory on the nature and method of inspiration. He simply affirmed his conviction that "the Scriptures are fully inspired and speak truth throughout." He distinguished between truth in substance and truth in statement and said that we must assume truth in statement as well as in substance. In a remarkably undogmatic statement, he declared that "whatever these inspired writers meant to say, or whatever we learn from subsequent revelation that God meant to say through their words . . . *that* we hold to be true, thoroughly true, not only in substance but in statement—unless the contrary can be shown."[3]

In a similar vein, Broadus said in his *Commentary on the Gospel of Matthew* of 1886 that Matthew and Luke cannot both be correct concerning the words spoken by the voice from heaven at Jesus' baptism, and that similar variations are found elsewhere. He gave three further examples and concluded that at least some of them cannot be harmonized. Although such facts do not contradict the complete inspiration of Scripture, Broadus explained, they "should make us cautious in theorizing as to verbal inspiration. . . ."[4]

On the other hand, language reflecting a developed doctrine of biblical inerrancy is to be found in two other founding professors at the seminary, Basil Manly, Jr., and James

3. John A. Broadus, *Three Questions As to the Bible* (Philadelphia: American Baptist Publication Society, 1883), 25, 26.

4. Broadus, *Commentary on the Gospel of Matthew* (Philadelphia: American Baptist Publication Society, 1886), 58.

P. Boyce, both of whom had been students at Princeton Seminary.

In his *The Bible Doctrine of Inspiration Explained and Vindicated,* published in 1888, Manly sums up his doctrine as: "The whole Bible is truly God's word written by men." It was important for him to disagree with much that historical criticism was affirming, for he believed that if the Pentateuch were not by Moses, then the history in it would not be true, and Jesus and his apostles would not be speaking truth. He would remove Daniel from the canon if the traditional views of authorship were not correct. He said the authorship of the fourth Gospel by the Apostle John is vital to the whole system of Christianity. And finally, Manly claimed that the statements of the Bible outside religion are true and that the Bible avoids any error when it deals with the many types of human life and knowledge which abound in it.[5]

James P. Boyce, founding president of the seminary, took a similar position. In the 1884 edition of his *Brief Catechism of Bible Doctrine,* he used the "dictation" theory as an analogy and affirmed that the Bible is exactly as God wished it "as much as if he had written every word himself," and it is to be believed and obeyed "as much so as though God had spoken directly to us."[6] In his *Abstract of Systematic Theology* of 1887, he said that it is only in the Bible that man finds a truth immune from "liability to error which arises from human imperfection."[7]

The Turn of the Century

At the turn of the century, a good many Southern Baptist leaders were beginning to acknowledge that a pietistic

5. Basil Manly, Jr., *The Bible Doctrine of Inspiration Explained and Vindicated* (New York: A. C. Armstrong and Son, 1888), 233, 234, 237, 248.

6. James P. Boyce, *Brief Catechism of Bible Doctrine* (Louisville: A. C. Caperton and Company, 1884), 5.

7. Boyce, *Abstract of Systematic Theology* (Philadelphia: American Baptist Publication Society, 1887), *vii.*

evangelical understanding of the Bible did not really depend upon insistence on detailed factual accuracy, and that application of human judgment had a place in biblical studies. Spokesmen were looking beyond the negative results of criticism and advocating a moderate approach.

In a 1901 *Seminary Magazine* article, W. O. Carver, professor at Southern Seminary (1896–1943), pointed out:

Biblical criticism is not the name of a cave of robbers or a den of thieves. It stands for a method and a sphere of study in the main desirable and serviceable, even essential to full truth. It has been occupied by men of various spirit, temperament, and ability. This is reason, not for deterring, but attracting competent seekers after truth, whatever their views of the methods and results of some Biblical critics.[8]

In that same year, E. Y. Mullins wrote in *The Task of the Theologian Today* that higher criticism is a method that can be used by conservative as well as liberal scholars: "It is certainly a fatal mistake in earnest people to deny the possibility of a method of Biblical research without peril to the faith, when the method in question seeks simply to ascertain the facts of the case."[9] In his later work, *The Christian Religion in Its Doctrinal Expression*, he declared that biblical authority does not preclude historical and scientific deviation from exact truth. "The biblical revelation is sufficient, certain, and authoritative for all religious ends. This means," Mullins went on, "the Bible meets all the requirements of the religious life of man as the inspired literary record of the self-revelation of God."[10]

8. W. O. Carver, "Wrong Ways of Meeting Destructive Criticism," *The Seminary Magazine* XIV (May, 1901), 339.
9. E. Y. Mullins, *The Task of the Theologian of Today* (Louisville: privately printed [n.d.]), 339.
10. Mullins, *The Christian Religion in Its Doctrinal Expression* (Philadelphia: Roger Williams Press, 1917), 151, 152; cf. 152, 153.

The Early Robertson

After he came to the seminary in 1885, Robertson absorbed in a rather normal fashion the conservatism of Manly. After all, Manly taught the course in biblical introduction in which critical matters were treated in Robertson's day; and this course provided the critical framework for Robertson's early study, teaching, and writing. Robertson even took over the course in biblical introduction in 1892 when Manly died.

An instructive example of Robertson's early position is his statement on "The Relative Authority of Scripture and Reason" at the Baptist Congress of 1892. Throughout the Congress, many of the men from northern institutions had expressed their willingness to accept some of the newer critical methods and conclusions in their study of the Bible. Robertson apparently was surprised by what he had heard, for he began: "I had a sort of speech in my head when I left Louisville, but so many things have been put into it since coming here that I do not know whether I have much of a speech in it now." Then he defended the inerrancy of the Bible—that is, "the inerrancy of God's original Scriptures," for Robertson acknowledged that there are "minor" discrepancies in the writings people now have.[11]

The Mature Robertson

In 1895 Robertson succeeded Broadus as professor of New Testament interpretation and moved from his work in biblical introduction (which he had been doing in addition to assisting Broadus with work in the New Testament). He also moved more consciously to a dynamic view of the nature of the authority of the Bible. In direct confrontation with the biblical text and released from the need to provide a rationale for a given view of inspiration and authority,

---

11. A. T. Robertson, "The Relative Authority of Scripture and Reason," in *Proceedings of the Baptist Congress* (New York: Baptist Congress Publishing Company, 1892), 186, 192.

Robertson moderated his position. At about the same time, he also married Broadus's daughter. Frank Stagg, Emeritus Professor of New Testament at Southern Seminary, comments that the spirited Ella Broadus

> . . . was a match for her distinguished father and her husband. She was a scholar and servant of Christ in her own right. She doubtless supported her "Archibald" in his decisive move away from the restrictive posture of Basil Manly, Jr., toward the openness of Broadus in regard to their view of the Bible. . . . Robertson followed Broadus, not Manly, and thus helped Southern Baptists see scholarship as friend, and not foe, to authentic biblical study.[12]

Do not misunderstand me. Robertson was not a flaming liberal. He followed the practice of accepting critical results as they could be adjusted to his views of the divine authority of Scripture; but those critical results enabled him to get beyond a superficial, "statement of the facts" view, to a deeper view of the Bible's authority and significance. After several years, he accepted the view that the relationship between Matthew and Mark resulted from Matthew's knowledge and use of Mark. He used that theory in his 1911 commentary on Matthew, which was published in a series edited by Shailer Mathews of the University of Chicago.[13]

In his 1924 volume entitled *The Christ of the Logia*, Robertson expressed his conviction that the non-Markan material common to Matthew and Luke comes from a common sayings source which he called the "Logia," a hypothetical source generally called "Q." He made a distinction between

12. Frank Stagg, "A. T. Robertson: Shaper of New Testament Studies," a pamphlet in the 1987 series *Shapers of Southern Baptist Heritage* (Historical Commission of the Southern Baptist Convention, 901 Commerce Street, Nashville, Tennessee 37203-3620).

13. Robertson, *Commentary on the Gospel According to Matthew*, in *The Bible for Home and School*, Shailer Mathews, ed., (New York: Macmillan, 1911).

the presentation of Jesus Christ in the "Logia" and in the other sources.[14]

Today we would speak of Robertson's method as a conservative "redaction-critical" approach to the various sources. He also expressed his view with regard to another of the methods characteristic of the higher criticism of the Bible. In a review of a work on form criticism in the *Review and Expositor* in 1933, he claimed that form criticism "is legitimate and helpful if pursued with patience and wisdom."[15]

The change in Robertson's attitude toward the Bible is to be seen mainly in what he did not do: He refused to align himself with the exclusiveness and imperialism which showed itself in fundamentalism.[16] An article by Robertson on "The Bible as Authority" in 1922 gives positive evidence of Robertson's moderation. He affirmed that he continued to think of the authority of the Bible as being the authority of God. But he said:

> The essential problem about the Bible is not whether this detail of history has been established by research or whether this allusion in popular language to matter in nature is in harmony with modern scientific theory, which is constantly shifting its form of expression. That is quite beside the problem of the Bible. The authority relates to God's revelation of himself to men and to man's relation to God.[17]

Robertson was discovering that something more must be made of Broadus's distinction between truth in substance and truth in statement. In his earlier view, stated at the Baptist Congress of 1892, of course, any lack of inerrancy in statement resulted from the fact that we do not have the original

14. Robertson, *The Christ of the Logia* (Nashville: Sunday School Board of the Southern Baptist Convention, 1924).

15. Robertson, Review of *The Formation of the Gospel Tradition* by Vincent Taylor, *Review and Expositor* (October, 1933), 467.

16. Beale, 29.

17. Robertson, "The Bible as Authority," *The Homiletic Review* LXXXIII (February, 1922), 103.

documents. In the 1922 statement, however, Robertson acknowledged that a lack of conformity or inerrancy in statement may result from constantly shifting forms of statement. Truthfulness in religious substance does not require conformity in scientific statement.[18]

Robertson's pilgrimage was made within the Baptist fellowship, of course, and his modifications created difficulties for some in the fellowship who were slow in accommodating their understanding of the authority of the Bible to such things as documentary relationships and the distinction between form and substance. Indeed, I. J. Van Ness of the Southern Baptist Sunday School Board wrote to Robertson in 1911 that his acceptance of the two-source hypothesis in the commentary on Matthew would "destroy any real inspiration in the Book of Matthew."[19]

Numerous sharp letters passed between Van Ness and Robertson.[20] Finally, Robertson assured Van Ness that decisions in the area of Gospel relationships are tentative, and that Robertson was not omniscient. Van Ness apparently concluded that he was not omniscient either. They agreed to work together in the Baptist fellowship in disagreement on that point. What a tragedy if Robertson's career had been cut short in 1911!

Searching for Higher Ground

Robertson's position is one that allows differences—not because he refused to take a stand, but because a higher ground makes the opposing positions relative. This higher ground is the experience of the trustworthiness of the Bible as it is used to proclaim the good news and enable hearers to experience God's grace.

I believe it can be shown that Robertson's churchmanship,

18. Ibid.
19. Letter from I. J. Van Ness to Robertson, May 2, 1911, on file in the library of the Southern Baptist Theological Seminary, Louisville, Kentucky.
20. Correspondence on file in Southern Seminary library.

or more particularly, his preaching as an expression of his churchmanship, is the high ground from which all of his work makes sense. The multitude of books he wrote do not constitute attempts to contribute to scholarship in the first instance, but to preaching. His wedding of criticism and exegesis was directed by preaching. To approach his expository work, character studies, and even *Word Pictures*[21] as scholarship is to miss the point. He even approached Greek grammar from his vocation as a minister.

Robertson's conviction about the importance of the close reading of the text with attention to the fine nuances, for example, was the attitude of a preacher. He thought of himself first and foremost as a preacher. In an interview for *The Baptist Student* magazine in May 1932, Frank Leavell asked Robertson which of the three kinds of service was the highest, preaching, teaching, or writing. Robertson replied, "Preaching! Yes, preaching is the greatest work in the world. The element in the other two that makes them worthwhile is the preaching that they contain." He went on and declared that he had never considered himself anything other than a preacher. He pointed to the massive *Grammar of the Greek New Testament in the Light of Historical Research* in particular and stated that his major idea in it was to help men to preach the Word.[22]

It is obvious today that as individuals and as denominations, we need high ground. We need a perspective and a compelling vision that allow the different gifts of men and women in our fellowship to fit into proper place—the same sort of high ground that allowed space for the Southern Baptist Sunday School Board official and A. T. Robertson in 1911. The career of A. T. Robertson may point us to that high ground.

21. Robertson, *Word Pictures in the New Testament*, 6 volumes (Nashville: Sunday School Board of the Southern Baptist Convention, 1930–1933).
22. Frank H. Leavell, "Archibald Thomas Robertson, An Interview for Students," *The Baptist Student* 10 (May 1932), 3.

8

E. Y. Mullins: The Bible's Authority Is a Living, Transforming Reality

RUSSELL H. DILDAY, JR.

(Printed by permission of the Historical Commission, Southern Baptist Convention°)

Editor's Introduction

Sometimes the right person finds the right author to tell his story. That seems to have happened in this chapter. It is the story of E. Y. Mullins, president of Southern Baptist Seminary (1899–1928) as related by the current president of the world's largest seminary, Southwestern.

Because President Dilday has had to lead his institution during the controversy of the 1980s, we would expect him to have a special "feel" for the way Mullins had to contend with the similar conflict of the 1920s. We are not disappointed. The earlier controversy is an inevitable part of the Mullins story, and Dilday tells it well.

But the dominant notes in this story are positive. And Dr. Dilday is equipped to deal with them. Not only did he write his 1960 doctoral dissertation on Mullins.[1] He has also managed, during an incredibly demanding career of pastoral and

---

°This chapter, which begins on page 109, appears by permission of the executive director of the Historical Commission of the Southern Baptist Convention. Though it is considerably longer, it is similar at several points to "E. Y. Mullins: Shaper of Theology," a pamphlet in *Shapers of Southern Baptist Heritage* (Nashville: Historical Commission of the Southern Baptist Convention, 1987), by Russell H. Dilday, Jr.

1. Russell Dilday, "The Apologetic Method of E. Y. Mullins" (unpublished Th.D. dissertation, 1960, Southwestern Baptist Theological Seminary Library, Forth Worth, Texas).

denominational leadership, to "keep up his homework." In that respect also he is like Mullins, "a man of books and a man of the people."[2]

How the Bible "Gets Inside People"

What did Mullins offer that is so important today for dealing with the Bible? To use his own words, he regarded the Bible "as a living thing, like an organism, full of life and power, instinct [or infused] with the life of the God of human experience." This means, as Dilday states Mullins' view, that "the Bible is authoritative because it leads persons to God through Christ and relates them to redemptive forces." Thus, as Dilday also says, "External authority in Jesus Christ and the Scriptures is constantly in the process of becoming internal as men appropriate Christ."

We might put that in the following way. Christ and Scripture gain preeminence even within our inner, spontaneous lives.

Should we call this kind of view "subjectivist"?[3] At the 1987 Ridgecrest Conference on Inerrancy, distinguished historian Mark Noll treated Mullins in a very sympathetic way. At one point, referring to schools of thought early in this century, the Wheaton College professor said Mullins made use of a "subjectivist" philosophy.[4]

This could be misleading, however, since the term is used so often today to refer to views which dismiss all objective, external criteria of truth. Consider Mullins' statement, which Dilday quotes: "Experience would ever go astray without the ever-present corrective influence of the Scriptures, and the authority of the Scripture would never become for us a vital

---

2. William E. Ellis, *"A Man of Books and a Man of the People": E. Y. Mullins and the Crisis of Moderate Southern Baptist Leadership* (Macon, Ga.: Mercer, 1985).

3. Essentially that criticism was made of Mullins at the Ridgecrest conference by Richard Land of Criswell College when Land compared "a Mullins-type fideistic affirmation of Scripture's veracity" unfavorably with the strict inerrantist, Princeton view of Scripture. Richard D. Land, "Response," in *Proceedings of the Conference on Biblical Inerrancy 1987* (Nashville: Broadman, 1987), Michael A. Smith, ed., 39.

4. Mark Noll, "A Brief History of Inerrancy, Mostly in America," in *Proceedings*, 18.

and transforming reality apart from the working of God's redeeming grace in us."

In light of such statements, Dilday is surely correct that
Mullins' idea of authority is a *balance* "between objectivity and
subjectivity. Christian experience is not an orphan," Dilday adds.
"It is grounded in the objective Word of God."[5]

I may be biased, since my minister father studied under
Mullins and I absorbed many of Mullins' ideas in my early years.
But it seems to me we might commend Mullins, not criticize
him, for being so confident that the objective biblical Word
does take root inside of people, livingly. And that it transforms
them.

A Pietist Approach

It is not quite the case that Southern Baptists are "Mullins-
ites" in their view of Scripture. There is no single person who
presides over their tradition in the way Luther presides, for example, over the tradition that bears his name. But, so far as the
approach to the Bible is concerned, no one in this century comes
closer than Mullins to filling that role.

Dilday believes that Mullins has influenced many, and that
he is also representative of many others, who together have
given Southern Baptists a distinctive form of mainstream-con-
servative view. How should we characterize this Mullins-type
approach? The term *pietist* probably creates fewer misunderstandings than most other terms we could use. That is what
Clark Pinnock of McMaster Divinity College had in mind when
he spoke at Ridgecrest of "simple biblicism" (explained in the
Introduction to this book). Mullins fits very naturally into that
category. He clearly avoided any detailed inerrancy doctrine
and thus steered clear of Pinnock's alternative category,
"elaborate biblicism."

Another thinker who provided a way to understand Mullins'
position is Mark Noll. Author of an important book on the

---

5. Dilday's point was reinforced at Ridgecrest by J. Leo Garrett,
whose seminar paper showed that Mullins rejected, and was rejected by,
both a rationalistic, scholastic, and fundamentalist group, and by a subjectivist, liberal, and authority-denying group. James Leo Garrett, Jr., "The
Teaching of Recent Southern Baptist Theologians on the Bible," in *Proceedings*, 293, 294.

subject,[6] Noll presented at Ridgecrest a scheme of four ways in which conservative evangelicals have responded to the situation created by modern higher criticism of the Bible. For our purposes it is important that Noll, himself an inerrantist, views each of these "four ways" as a means of defending "a fully truthful Bible."

Noll called one of his four ways the "Baptist" way, although he pointed out that this same approach is found also in Holiness, Pentecostal, and Wesleyan circles. It affirms the truthfulness of the Bible, not on the basis of rational arguments, but on the basis of the Bible's inwardly experienced truth. Noll featured Mullins as the most influential advocate of this approach among Baptists in the South.

The pietist quality of this approach sets it off sharply from the "Princeton Presbyterian" view, which was another of Noll's "four ways." And the same quality also appears to set the Baptist approach off from another of Noll's "four ways," namely, the "dispensational/fundamentalist" approach. That view defends the literal truth of each biblical detail by means of a complex scheme of different historical periods.

On the other hand, the pietist character of the Baptist approach aligns it fairly closely *with* the position of British evangelicals. Their approach constitutes Noll's fourth way of defending a fully truthful Bible.[7]

As both Noll and Land pointed out at Ridgecrest, elements of all four of Noll's approaches may be found among Southern Baptists.[8] Nevertheless, the analyses of Noll, Dilday, and Pinnock seem to converge upon the conclusion that none of the other three ways can approach the "Baptist" way—which is also Mullins' way—as the typical way in which Southern Baptists use the Bible and maintain its truthfulness.

Infallible on Matters It Purposes to Address

One final idea of Mullins' that requires notice—both because it is important and because it has been ignored, if not obscured,

6. *Between Faith and Criticism: Evangelicals, Scholarship, and the Bible in America* (Society of Biblical Literature, Centennial Publication Project: Harper & Row, 1987).
7. Noll, 13, 18, 19; cf. 13–21.
8. Ibid., 21, and Land, "Response," 34, 35.

in some circles—is that the Bible's infallibility pertains specifically to the religious purpose for which it exists.

Mullins states this idea in a crucial passage in *The Christian Religion in Its Doctrinal Expression* of 1917, where he uses an apt quotation from Marcus Dods to make his point. Dilday quotes from this passage late in the chapter that follows. He could hardly avoid it, since the passage is the single place in Mullins' major systematic work that is indexed under, "Bible, infallibility of."[9]

Yet this crucial passage is never mentioned in a 1980 volume by Bush and Nettles, *Baptists and the Bible.* This is baffling, given the fact that Bush and Nettles give fourteen pages to Mullins, more than to any other, a fourth of that devoted to Mullins' chief systematic work.[10] The omission is serious because *Baptists and the Bible* provides Southern Baptist fundamental-conservatives with their standard picture, so to speak, of the views of Scripture which Baptists have historically held.[11]

This matter is not a scholarly quibble. The Mullins idea that tends to get lost in this way appears also in Southern Baptists' confessional statement, *The Baptist Faith and Message.* And it was through Mullins that it got there. Mullins chaired the committee that drew up the original *Baptist Faith and Message* of 1925. His idea that the Bible's infallibility had to do specifically with *religious* matters—or with "faith and practice" matters— was already present in previous Baptist confessions.[12]

The Mullins committee proceeded to make this idea clear in their new statement by adding the word "religious" to the language they found in the 1833 *New Hampshire Confession,*

9. E. Y. Mullins, *The Christian Religion in Its Doctrinal Expression.* The index reference on p. 505 refers to p. 152.

10. Bush and Nettles, *Baptists and the Bible* (Chicago: Moody Press, 1980), 285–300, cf. 294–297. Bush and Nettles appear to allude to the crucial passage in paragraph three, p. 298, without citing it. But if so, they do not fall far short of reversing the point Mullins was making.

11. Paige Patterson urged the book on me in these terms in a discussion and lengthy correspondence, June–November, 1985. Former Convention President James Draper also used the book as the basis for the historical part of his polemical book, *Authority: The Crucial Issue for Southern Baptists* (Old Tappan, N. J.: Revell, 1984), 4.

12. G. Hugh Wamble shows this in "The Background and Meaning of the 1963 Southern Baptist Articles of Faith on the Bible" in *Proceedings,* 346–48.

which was their basis. The resulting clause speaks as follows: the Bible is "the supreme standard by which all human conduct, creeds and *religious* opinions should be tried." That language remains unchanged in the current *Baptist Faith and Message* of 1963.[13]

These introductory remarks suggest some of the reasons E. Y. Mullins is a force to be reckoned with. But there are many more, as Russell Dilday makes clear in the immensely important essay which follows.

In the pamphlet files of the Southern Baptist Theological Seminary library are copies of three Louisville, Kentucky newspapers dated November 23, 1928. All three gave top headlines to the announcement of the death of E. Y. Mullins, who had been president of the seminary from 1899 until his death, and also president of the Baptist World Alliance and the Southern Baptist Convention.

The headline of *The Louisville Times*, bright red and one-inch high, read, "DEATH ENDS MULLINS' SERVICE." Page after page carried tributes from pastors of leading evangelical churches, bishops of the Roman Catholic Church, Jewish rabbis, mayors, judges, businessmen, club women, university professors, and politicians.

In one obituary Mullins was praised as a preacher, teacher, administrator, and a "liberator of men's minds from dogmatism." Tributes from around the world proved how widespread was the influence of this Southern Baptist theologian, philosopher, statesman, and pastor.

In this chapter, I want to explore this man's extraordinary religious leadership, especially with regard to his understanding of biblical authority.

13. *Annual of the SBC, 1963* (Nashville: Executive Committee of the Southern Baptist Convention, 1963), 270, emphasis added. In this place the 1925 and 1963 versions of Article I are printed side by side. For the *New Hampshire*, see William L. Lumpkin, *Baptist Confessions of Faith* (Philadelphia: Judson Press, 1959), 361, 362.

The Context: Controversy Among the Baptists

Denominationally, the period of American history during which Mullins was president of Southern Seminary was dominated by what has been called the "Modernist-Fundamentalist" controversy, a struggle which embroiled most denominations in fierce debates over such issues as the authority of Scripture, the relationship of faith and science, the supernatural elements in the Bible, higher criticism, and comparative religions.

Among Baptists during the first part of the twentieth century there were, according to historian A. H. Newman, three major parties. At one extreme, with their impressive academic strength, were those considered "liberals." By World War I, most of the Baptist seminaries in the North, including Colgate, Rochester, and the Baptist Divinity School at the University of Chicago, had adopted "liberal" positions.[1]

At the other extreme were the fundamentalists, whom Newman characterized as anti-intellectual and uncompromising concerning Scripture. Equating biblical higher criticism with the devil, many of them deserted their denominations and began to work primarily through independent, parachurch agencies and Bible institutes.

In the middle, still in control of the working forces of most denominations during this period, according to Newman, was a "moderate conservative" party.[2] With similar characteristics, these same parties have risen again in the theological controversies of our day.

In the Southern Baptist Convention, the issues being debated in Mullins' time sound remarkably familiar. Debates

1. George M. Marsden, *Fundamentalism and American Culture* (New York: Oxford University Press, 1980), 105.
2. A. H. Newman, "Recent Tendencies in Theology of Baptists," *American Journal of Theology* X (1906): 600–609.

then focused on such things as Baptist origins,[3] faith and science (the evolution controversy), biblical authority, creedalism, inspiration, and inerrancy. There were also accusations of liberalism in the seminaries, political conspiracies to control the convention by electing trustees of agencies, confrontations of fundamentalists and moderate conservatives, threats to withhold funds from the agencies, and conflicts over church-state issues, "the social gospel," and ecumenism.

As such issues were debated among Baptists in the North, "liberal," "moderate," and "fundamentalist" factions developed. But in the South, only "fundamentalists" and "moderates" contended for control of the denominational direction and machinery. A "liberal" or "modernist" party was virtually nonexistent among Southern Baptists. Those whom fundamentalists identified as Southern Baptist "modernists" in Mullins' time (and probably since) were actually "moderate conservatives."

A Model of Leadership

Because the issues he faced were so similar to those confronting Southern Baptists and others today, Mullins' scholarly, conservative, centrist method of dealing with them provides a timely model for denominational leadership today. His method represents the unique "mainstream" historic Baptist approach. Mullins became a spokesman for what was called the "moderate conservative" faction, rejecting modernism on the left with its disavowal of supernaturalism, and rejecting fundamentalism on the right with its scholastic reliance on reason.[4]

3. A controversy arose among Southern Baptists when William Whitsitt, president of Southern Seminary 1895–1899, showed that Baptist beginnings cannot be documented earlier than the seventeenth century.

4. William E. Ellis, *A Man of Books and a Man of the People* (Macon, Georgia: Mercer University Press, 1985), 41, x.

Since the link between fundamentalism and rationalism may be surprising to some readers, it deserves comment. Both in Mullins' time and today, one of the strongest forces shaping extreme fundamentalist views of the Bible has been the "Princeton theology" of Hodge, Alexander, and Warfield. This theology is based, in part, on widely held tenets of Scottish Common Sense Realism—for example, that truth is adequately supported only when it is based on the exact apprehensions of intellect, not on indefinable feelings. For the Princeton theologians, genuine religious experience grows out of right ideas. Right ideas, in turn, can be expressed only in words. On this basis, the Princetonians emphasized verbal inspiration and the inerrancy of Scripture in matters of historical detail, and tended to leave out the subjective element of the human author altogether. They believed faith must be grounded in right reason.[5] "It is the distinction of Christianity," Warfield wrote in 1903, "that it has come into the world clothed with the mission to *reason* its way to its dominion. . . . It is solely by reasoning that it has come thus far on its way to its kingship. And it is solely by reasoning that it will put all its enemies under its feet."[6]

Though Mullins believed human rational ability is generally trustworthy, he thought it was so clouded by sin that it cannot come to ultimate truth except by an experience of grace. Man knows ultimate truth not just by a priori reasoning, but by the entire personality, will, and emotion as well.

Mullins was neither a hardened traditionalist nor a faddish liberal, but a critical conservative who sought to communicate the Christian faith in contemporary terms.[7] While he stood strongly for the fundamental doctrines of evangelical theology and was enlisted to write one of the

5. Marsden, 111.

6. Benjamin Warfield, "Introduction" to Francis R. Beattie, *Apologetics* (Richmond, Virginia, 1903), x.

7. Timothy George, "Systematic Theology at Southern Seminary," *The Review and Expositor* LXXXII (1985): 37.

"Fundamentalist" tracts,[8] he refused to be pigeonholed or arbitrarily labeled by any faction.

On the one hand, there could be no doubt about E. Y. Mullins' strong opposition to theological liberalism. In his inaugural address he graphically described the liberalism then prevalent in sections of the theological world by saying its "coat of arms" symbolized doubt exultant over established doctrine.[9] Concerned that such liberalism could dilute the biblical faith of Southern Baptists, Mullins in 1915 summarized the tenets of liberal theology:

1. Biblical miracles are interpreted to bring them within the range of natural law or else are dismissed as unhistorical.

2. The narratives of the virgin birth, resurrection and other miracles were produced by "literary inventiveness."

3. The Bible writers were no more inspired than other literary composers.

4. Religion cannot be derived from external authority; it must answer to the highest intellectual demands of the age.

5. The personality of Christ belongs wholly in the natural sphere; he was unique only in his superior spiritual life.

6. The pre-existent Christ of Paul and John are products of primitive interpretation.

7. The resurrection was due to psychic experiences or visions and is not based on objective fact. So also the other miracles are to be explained in terms of religious psychology.

8. Jesus did not set himself forth as an object of worship; only a religious example.[10]

The president of Southern Seminary also spoke out intelligently against the negative influences of naturalistic

8. E. Y. Mullins, "The Testimony of Christian Experience," in *The Fundamentals* (Los Angeles: The Bible Institute, 1917), Volume 4, 314–323.

9. *The Baptist Argus* (Louisville, Kentucky), n.d., 8. Cited in Russell Dilday, "The Apologetic Method of E. Y. Mullins" (unpublished Th.D. dissertation, 1960, Southwestern Baptist Theological Seminary Library, Fort Worth, Texas), 15.

10. Mullins, "The Jesus of Liberal Theology," *The Review and Expositor* XII (1915): 175.

evolution, rationalistic higher criticism, and the unbiblical tenets of Rauschenbusch's social gospel. He believed such liberal inroads called for a scholarly restatement of biblical authority.

But on the other hand, Mullins strongly opposed the legalistic, rationalistic position of the fundamentalists, which he also saw as a serious threat to Southern Baptist theology. He objected when fundamentalists from the seminary board set up what came to be called a "smelling committee" to periodically visit faculty members in their search for heresy.[11]

During debates within the Southern Baptist Convention, he openly worked toward the "defeat of Radicals and Extremists . . . who want to put the thumb screws on everybody who does not agree in every detail with their statements of doctrine."[12] He described the fundamentalists as "hyperorthodox," "ultra-brethren," "lacking in common sense," and on another occasion, "big 'F' fundamentalists who agitated for control of the Convention and sought to 'harass and muzzle teachers in our schools.'"[13]

Rebuking one extremist he wrote, "Some of you brethren who train with the radical fundamentalists are going over on Catholic ground and leaving the Baptist position. A man who tries to pin his brethren down to stereotyped statements, such as your letter contains, has missed the Baptist spirit."[14]

While Mullins was not able to shape a moderate conservative consensus that would successfully bring together Southern Baptists on the left and the right, he did help the denomination avoid a serious schism during this troublesome period. He was called upon to chair the committee that successfully framed in 1925 the first statement of faith ever adopted by the Convention, "The Baptist Faith and

11. Ellis, 54.
12. Mullins, letter to Livingston Johnson, July 3, 1925. This letter and those cited subsequently are on file in the library of Southern Baptist Theological Seminary, Louisville, Ky.
13. Mullins, letters to George C. McDaniel, July 25, 1925; April 30, 1926.
14. Mullins, letter to J. Frank Norris, April 16, 1926.

Message," a statement little changed in the 1963 revision which is current today.

In addition, through his widespread, respected leadership in every area of denominational life, he helped his fellow Southern Baptists maintain organizational unity until the controversies of the twenties diminished.

A Historic Position on the Issues

Mullins' moderate conservative view represented what I believe has been the historic Baptist position on faith and science when he spoke to the evolution controversy. Of course he objected to the naturalism of certain scientific theories in his day, and was critical of "scientism" which elevated science to the place of ultimate authority. But Mullins did not feel the Christian faith was threatened by the various evolutionary hypotheses.

He believed science and philosophy have their own fields and purposes and should be allowed the freedom to investigate within their realms. But the purpose of Christianity is different. That purpose is to provide for the moral and spiritual needs of mankind. It was imperative, he felt, that both scientists and theologians recognize this division of labor.

On one occasion when a group of enthusiasts proposed making Bible reading compulsory in the public schools by legislative act, in traditional Baptist fashion Mullins countered that the Bible could be read in the classroom if no one objected. However, the reading must be free of any form of "compulsion."[15]

In the same vein, Mullins took the moderate conservative position in defending the responsible use of biblical criticism in the study of the Word of God. Recognizing the destructive potential of critics who approached the Bible from an antisupernaturalistic bias, he nevertheless acknowledged that higher criticism in the hands of reverent scholarship could be helpful. The authority of Scripture was not threatened by open investigation of authorship, date, or text.

15. Mullins, letter to Thomas E. Boorde, May 8, 1924.

As a moderate conservative Mullins faulted both fundamentalists and liberals for their extremism which led to name calling rather than fruitful communication. He represented the historical Baptist approach when he declared, "The really safe leaders of thought, however, are between the extremes. They are men who have sympathy on the one hand with those who are perplexed by the difficulties to faith occasioned by modern science and philosophy, and on the other hand are resolved to be loyal to Christ and His gospel."[16]

Threats to Biblical Authority from Two Sides

Mullins lived in a day when liberal theologians were rejecting the authority of the Bible in increasing numbers, some turning to the authority of human reason, others to an empirical, subjective religious consciousness. Pointing to the fact that human sin distorted man's understanding, Mullins rejected the authority of human reason as undependable. He also dismissed religious consciousness as sole authority because it reduced authority to the subjective level of anything anyone wanted to believe.

Mullins also defended the authority of the Bible against those who used the techniques of naturalistic higher criticism to deny the Bible's authenticity. He accused these unbelieving critics of approaching the Bible with preconceived ideas that ignore the facts supplied by the Bible itself. Although no Christian should expect the Bible to be exempt from even the most rigorous examination, the best approach, according to Mullins, is a sound, historical literary investigation combined with a spiritual appreciation for the contents of the Bible.

Stressing that the Bible writers employed the language and literary forms in common use in their own age (such as parable, allegory, and history), Mullins taught that some of the Bible's passages must be interpreted literally and others figuratively, depending on the type of literary genre. Jesus Christ

16. Mullins, *The Axioms of Religion* (Philadelphia: The Judson Press, 1901), 8.

is the core and center of revelation in the Scriptures, and therefore the ultimate principle by which the Bible is to be interpreted.

In addition to the assault from liberal theologians, Mullins believed there was also a serious challenge to orthodoxy from the extreme right where true biblical authority was being threatened by the rigid creedalism of the radical fundamentalists. In response, he strongly repudiated creedalism saying, "No creed can be set up as final and authoritative apart from the Scriptures."[17] He was willing, however, to identify certain essential truths for teachers to affirm before they were employed in schools of his own denomination:

> The Bible is God's revelation of himself through men moved by the Holy Spirit, and is our sufficient, certain and authoritative guide in religion. Jesus Christ was born of the Virgin Mary through the power of the Holy Spirit. He was the divine and eternal Son of God. He wrought miracles, healing the sick, casting out demons, raising the dead. He died as the vicarious atoning Saviour of the world and was buried. He ascended to the right hand of the Father. He will come again in person, the same Jesus who ascended from the Mount of Olives.[18]

Mullins saw the fundamentalist view of the Bible as rigid and mechanical. A better approach was the inductive view which regards the Bible "as a living thing, like an organism, full of life and power, instinct [infused] with the life of the God of human experience."[19] This inductive approach, that is, letting the Bible speak for itself rather than imposing on the Bible a preconceived rationalistic scheme, was apparent in Mullins' discussion of biblical authority. He criticized the traditional fundamentalist view as scholastic:

17. Mullins, *Baptist Beliefs* (Philadelphia: The American Baptist Publication Society, 1912), 7. Cited in Dilday, 65.

18. An address published in the *Annual of the SBC*, 1923, as quoted in L. Russ Bush and Tom J. Nettles, *Baptists and the Bible* (Chicago: Moody Press, 1980), 289, 290.

19. Mullins, *Freedom and Authority in Religion* (Philadelphia: Griffith and Rowland Press, 1913), 382.

It begins with an abstract principle not derived from Scripture, which conceives of the Biblical writers as mere unintelligent instruments or pens used by the Holy Spirit to dictate the truths of revelation. The Bible speaks, according to this view, with equal authority on science and related subjects as upon religion. A single mistake in matters of science would invalidate the authority of the Bible. Even the Hebrew vowel points were inspired of God in the Old Testament equally with the consonants and the language generally.[20]

Obviously, Mullins could not be categorized with those who accept the Hodge-Warfield-Lindsell doctrine of biblical inerrancy in all historical, geographical, and scientific matters. While he believed the Bible did not mislead us in these matters, the better view, according to Mullins, was the inductive view that:

. . . refuses to adopt any abstract or *a priori* starting point, but rather goes directly to the Bible itself for the evidence of its own inspiration. Its watchword is conformity to the testimony of Scripture as to the inspiration of Scripture. In other words, it gathers the data from the Bible and on them builds up its view of the authority of the Bible. This view recognizes that God was in the history as well as in the literature; that he spoke to Israel through the prophets; that Jesus Christ is the supreme and final revelation of God; that miracles and the supernatural must be admitted as part of God's method of revelation; that the Scriptures are the final and sufficient and authoritative record of God's revelation and that when we have correctly interpreted the Scriptures we have found God's truth for our religious life.[21]

The Bible's Living, Transforming Authority

Rejecting inadequate alternatives, Mullins centered authority in the will of God, which is embodied in Jesus Christ, who therefore is the absolute religious authority. The

20. Ibid., 379.
21. Ibid., 280.

authority of Jesus is expressed historically and objectively in the Scriptures, so that the Bible also is identified as our authority. Speaking for the Protestant tradition generally, as well as for his own tradition, he wrote:

> For Baptists there is one authoritative source of religious truth and knowledge. It is to that source they look in all matters relating to doctrine, to policy, to the ordinances, to worship, and to Christian living. That source is the Bible.[22]

Mullins made it clear that the Bible is authoritative because it leads persons to God through Christ and relates them to redemptive forces.

> The Scriptures do not and cannot take the place of Jesus Christ. We are not saved by belief in the Scriptures, but by a living faith in Christ. To understand what is meant by the phrase the "authority of the Bible" we need only to remember that in so expressing ourselves we are not speaking *in vacuo* [in a vacuum], and apart from any sense of the function of a literature as distinct from that of a personal object in religion. The authority of Scripture is that simply of an inspired literature which interprets a life.[23]
>
> In short, Christ as the Revealer of God and Redeemer of men is the seat of authority in religion and above and underneath and before the Bible. But the Bible is the authoritative literature which leads us to Christ.[24]

Mullins linked Christian experience to his pattern of religious authority. Authority, rooted in the will of God, the person of Christ, and the Scriptures, is expressed internally in the believer's own experience of grace. This gives to Mullins' scheme of religious authority a balance between objectivity and subjectivity. Christian experience is not an orphan. It

22. Mullins, *Baptists and the Bible* (Nashville: The Sunday School Board of the SBC, n.d.), 3. Cited in Dilday, 67.
23. Mullins, *Freedom and Authority in Religion*, 393.
24. Ibid., 394.

is not an independent and isolated source of truth. It is grounded in the objective Word of God.

For Mullins, revelation and Christian experience are eternally welded together. He sees revelation as the force which, through the power of the Holy Spirit, brings one to truth as that person meets the Author of revelation personally in Christian experience. Revelation always comes first—experience second. The two are complementary expressions of the same body of truth.[25]

External authority in Jesus Christ and the Scriptures is constantly in the process of becoming internal as men appropriate Christ. Mullins said: "Experience would ever go astray without the ever-present corrective influence of the Scriptures, and the authority of the Scripture would never become for us a vital [living] and transforming reality apart from the working of God's redeeming grace in us."[26]

This principle of authority avoids the weaknesses of the mechanical, legalistic type found in creedalism and bibliolatry. Conversely, it avoids the unsound conclusions of extreme individualism. The Scriptures are a corrective to unbridled experience, while experience gives life and meaning to the Scriptures.

Mullins preferred the dynamic theory of inspiration which maintains that the thought rather than the language was inspired. He believed the writers were enabled to declare truth unmixed with error but were permitted to convey their ideas in the forms of their own selection; therefore the Bible is both a divine and a human book. Mullins was quick to add, however, that no theory can adequately explain inspiration.[27]

The authority of the Bible according to Mullins was not based on abstract, rational theories but on the Bible's function and purpose. This functional authority of the Bible is

25. Mullins, *The Christian Religion in Its Doctrinal Expression* (Philadelphia: The Judson Press, 1954), 77.

26. Ibid., 27.

27. Ibid., 144.

affirmed by an inductive study that takes into account all the facts of Scripture and experience and lets them speak for themselves.

> We must let the Bible tell its own story and not hold it to false standards and tests. The Bible then is a book of religion, not of science. As such it has proved hitherto and will continue to prove in the future, man's sufficient and authoritative guide. It is a vital living authority, and not a mechanical and ecclesiastical one.[28]

The infallibility of the Bible is therefore determined by function, not by scholastic theories. Mullins quoted Marcus Dods favorably:

> What is the infallibility we claim for the Bible? Is it infallibility in grammar, in style, in science, or what? Its infallibility must be determined by its purpose. If you say that your watch is infallible, you mean, as a timepiece; not that it has a flawless case, not that it will tell you the day of the month, or predict tomorrow's weather.[29]

The Impact of Mullins' View of the Bible

Mullins' influence on later Southern Baptist thought is clear. His theological legacy was preserved through two of his "disciples," W. T. Conner at Southwestern Baptist Theological Seminary and Harold W. Tribble, his successor in the chair of systematic theology at Southern.

Based on the assumption that Mullins' view is representative, it seems fair to draw the conclusion that Southern Baptist theologians have given their denomination a distinctive understanding of biblical authority. That distinction places them in the mainstream of conservative theology.

Reflecting the pattern of Mullins, Southern Baptists have avoided, for the most part, both extremes at either end of the

28. Ibid., p. 153.
29. Marcus Dods, "The Bible: Its Origin and Nature" (lectures delivered before Lake Forest College, Lake Forest, Illinois). Cited in Mullins, *The Christian Religion in Its Doctrinal Expression*, 152, 153.

theological spectrum regarding the Bible. They have rejected the liberal, humanistic position that makes the Bible little more than another ancient book, full of errors and contradictions, and therefore not authoritative. On the other hand they have rejected also the tendency to elevate the Bible to a level it never claims for itself, in some cases to a position even above God himself.

Mullins knew that, rightly understood, terms like infallibility and inerrancy can be posited for the Bible, but wrongly understood, these terms can create division and confusion. Ultrainerrantists, at times, advocate a rationally guaranteed perfection that makes human reason, not divine revelation, the final criterion. This creates an epistemological crutch, a pseudocertainty, which while it purports to erase doubts, actually inserts a humanly devised conceptual scheme to make the Scriptures do what man believes they should.

Southern Baptist theologians like Mullins have helped the members of that denomination retain the dynamic of divine revelation without separating it from the earthen vessel of the scriptural writings. Such theologians have reminded the constituency how important it is to recognize the element of mystery in the Bible which was reverently acknowledged by the church fathers and reformers. These Southern Baptist thinkers have also reaffirmed the valuable concept of the accommodation of the Holy Spirit to the limitations of human language, a fact Calvin emphasized so effectively. They have taught that the Bible is both rooted in the context of time and, at the same time, is timeless. Its ultimate authority is in its relation to the living Word. Understanding its truth thus requires a living faith in Christ through the work of the Holy Spirit.

Within the mainstream of conservative theology, Southern Baptist theologians for the most part have not followed the rationalistic approach, nor have they used the typical language of scholastic inerrancy. While giving the Bible its rightful place as the sole authority for faith and practice, they have based that authority on the Bible's internal description of its meaning and function rather than on some external theory of inspiration.

The Current Controversy Among Southern Baptists

The controversy over the Bible which has occupied Southern Baptists' attention in recent years can have some positive results. For example, should the denomination be straying from its commitment to the Bible as God's inspired Word and the authority for faith and practice, then the focus of the current debate surely would tend to draw it back.

The debate also has heightened interest in the Bible by encouraging new discussion, understanding, and proclamation of its truth. Everyone involved agrees that total and unreserved allegiance to the Bible is essential to the denomination's continued vitality and uniqueness. Thus even controversies, if they call people back to a healthy, revitalized biblical authority, can be of value.

But there are dangers in the controversy, too. The divisiveness, the party spirit, the loss of trust, the diversion from the denomination's main functions of evangelism and missions are all tragic results. In a 1906 address, Mullins warned that to put the chief stress on the question whether there is one Isaiah or two is "to assume that the Gospel is primarily a question of intellect and literary criticism, whereas it is primarily a question of sin and regeneration, of justification and redemption. . . . You will never run the train of missions and education through to the New Jerusalem of our hopes until you quit tinkering with the running gear."[30]

Already in the mid-1980s, Southern Baptist evangelism leaders were pointing to convention polarization as one of the reasons for a decline in baptisms. If discussions about the Bible cannot be carried out prayerfully and with a sense of humility, trust, and fellowship, all will be losers. Christians of all denominations can learn from E. Y. Mullins, who had little

30. Mullins, "Baptists and Higher Education in Kentucky" (an unpublished address, 1906), 18.

patience for what he called "abnormal doctrinal sensitiveness" which he encountered in certain of his brethren. "I maintain that I have no right to refuse to call a Baptist my brother merely because he does not happen to be my twin brother, and I also maintain that another Baptist has no right to refuse to call me brother (and nag and torment me) because I am not his twin."[31]

Southern Baptists can celebrate the fact that although there is theological diversity among them, there is practically total unanimity concerning their commitment to the Bible as the divinely inspired, sufficient, certain, and authoritative guide for faith and practice. No small part of this unanimity among Southern Baptists is the lasting legacy of E. Y. Mullins.

31. Ibid., 17.

9

W. T. Conner: Reason and Freedom, Not Inerrancy

STEWART A. NEWMAN

Editor's Introduction

In this chapter, Stewart A. Newman lets a profound and pre-possessing thinker, W. T. Conner, explain why the Bible's authority cannot be fully accepted apart from a free exercise of reason.

Conner's point will be clearer if we reflect on the fact that God makes us both rational and free. Our reason and freedom are therefore *parts of what we are*, as God has made us. If we were to embrace the Bible as God's authoritative Word with anything *less* than the full exercise of our reason, or in any way *other* than as free persons, we would be "holding out on God"— holding back part of what we are. We would be yielding in only a partial way to God, rendering less than our complete selves to him. It would be as though we first cut off an arm and a leg, and then said, "Here am I, O God. I give myself entirely to you." But God demands our all—heart, soul, strength, *and mind.*

Moreover, Conner believes human reason and conscience "will assert themselves against any authority that seeks to suppress them." They must do so, he argues, because "God himself is immanent in the reason and conscience of man, and the motive power of the universe is surging up in them to accomplish its eternal purpose."

"But," we might ask, "can anyone who accepts such a view embrace the Bible as authority?" The answer is that no one who *rejects* the view can accept the Bible as authority. The New Testament clearly teaches this view of reason and conscience (John 1:9, Rom. 2:15). And "the motive power of the universe" which surges up in our reason and conscience is a key part

of what the New Testament means by God's Logos or Word
(John 1:1–5, 9; see also Col. 1:16, 17).

Is Conner Also Among the Inerrantists?

Nothing I have said will prepare the reader, however, for the
remarkable passion with which Newman has written this chapter. He sounds like Paul in Galatians. Why such feeling?

Newman is Conner's former student, long-time colleague, and
biographer. And he has written this essay to correct a mistake
which could rob all of us, not just Southern Baptists, of an important figure out of our common Christian past—the real W. T.
Conner.

The beloved Conner, who was on the faculty of Southwestern
Seminary in Fort Worth from 1910 to 1949, is probably the
most influential theologian to have taught there. He is a major
force shaping the Southern Baptist tradition. Thus it is no sur-
prise that inerrantists want him on their side. In fact, several of
them have recently claimed him. It is *that claim* which has
prompted Newman, not to say "provoked" him, to write.

The trouble arose on a large scale in 1984 when James
Draper, then president of the Convention, published a small
book entitled *Authority*. In that book, Draper referred to "B. B.
Warfield . . . who was a champion of biblical authority and
inerrancy." Draper went on to say, in the very next syllable,
"Conner obviously agreed with Warfield."[1]

David Beale, a professor at Bob Jones University, seems to
have taken this glaring error as a fact in a book which was
widely circulated among Southern Baptists the next year. Beale
supplied no documentation on the point; but, in words that suggest dependence upon Draper, he declared that W. T. Conner
"during thirty-nine years of service wrote twelve books expressing his strong belief in the Bible's inerrancy and authority," and
that Conner "long defended the verbal inspiration and inerrancy of the Bible."[2]

---

1. James T. Draper, Jr., *Authority: The Critical Issue for Southern
Baptists* (Old Tappan, N. J.: Revell, 1984), p. 65.
2. David O. Beale, *SBC: House on the Sand?* (Greenville, S. C.: Unusual
Publications, c. 1985 Bob Jones University), pp. 52, 123. The book was
promoted vigorously in the Spring, 1985 issue of *The Southern Baptist*

Meanwhile, Draper's error concerning Conner had an even more important life of its own. In 1984, while Draper was still Convention president, his new book was mailed, free of charge, to some 35,000 Southern Baptist pastors. Someone was prepared to pay dearly to be sure Southern Baptists understood their past in a certain way.

No doubt Draper himself simply made a mistake. But how did it happen? The answer appears to lie in the same 1980 volume, *Baptists and the Bible,* which was discussed in the introduction to the previous chapter.[3] That book treats Conner and also a very different man, B. H. Carroll, in the same chapter. Carroll, founding president of Southwestern Seminary, was an awesome advocate of inerrancy and verbal inspiration. Referring to Carroll and Conner, *Baptists and the Bible* says, "Their statements on biblical inspiration are couched in somewhat dissimilar outward forms; yet the differences lie in the areas of emphasis and personal temperament rather than in essence."[4]

I do not see how that sentence can be defended. In any case, once the issue has been posed in that way, it is inevitable that many readers of *Baptists and the Bible* will read its account of Conner more or less as Draper seems to have read it, even though that account also quotes some choice passages from Conner.

What is the real W. T. Conner like? No one is better able to say than Stewart Newman.

This chapter is written in response to the effort by a small company of persons to impose their system of simplistic biblicism upon the work and works of W. T. Conner.[5] The authors who seek to use him in this fashion must have been born about the time he died (1952). They never saw him, and

Journal (P. O. Box 468, Buchanan, Georgia 30113), an issue which also carried a long, glowing review of the book by Harold Lindsell.

3. Compare L. Russ Bush and Tom J. Nettles, *Baptists and the Bible* (Chicago: Moody Press, 1980), 320, with Draper, *Authority,* 4, 64, 65.

4. *Baptists and the Bible,* 306. Contrast Conner's rather barbed comment about Carroll, quoted by Dr. Newman on pp. 131, 132.

5. I have asked Dr. James to incorporate the full documentation into his introduction to this chapter.

never heard him say a word. Yet they claim to know him and what he thought about the Bible as they read into his writings their own ideas of biblical revelation, trying to appropriate his good reputation as an ally of their cause.

Many of us did know Conner. We are prepared to reject the merest suggestion that he subscribed to the kind of biblicism these writers advocate. I am bold to speak for the large group who knew Conner, for I knew him very well, having been closely associated with him during the last half of his illustrious career, during the most mature years of his active life. For half a dozen years I was a student in his classes. I heard him discuss firsthand many of the ideas that this group of inerrantist writers proposes regarding the Bible.

For fifteen years I was associated with Conner as a member of the seminary faculty, and for much of that time we shared a joint office. I assisted him in the preparation of the manuscripts of his major works for publication. At times during his writing he became ill and despaired of his life. More than once he shared with me what he had in mind for the particular writing and asked that, in case he did not live, I should bring it to completion.

I knew Conner well and am prepared to contradict any who claim that his idea of the Bible coincided in any appreciable sense with these writers' notions of it. Because the ideas they now espouse were rather prevalent at the time, Conner devoted a disproportionate part of his classroom discussions to the refutation of these very notions. He did his best to lead the minds of his students beyond such easy, rulebook conceptions of the nature and use of the Book.

The concept of revelation was central to Conner's thought. For him the entire revelatory process, of which the Bible is but one part, consists always in a two-party transaction. Both God and man are inevitably involved in it. To underscore the point, he often quoted the simple aphorism: "The Bible is as much the Word of God as if man had nothing to do with it; the Bible is as much the words of men as if God had nothing to do with it." He had no patience with those who claim that it was

W. T. Conner: Reason and Freedom, Not Inerrancy

delivered to man by "being hidden under a rock in Missouri, or inscribed on golden plates and delivered by an angel to a farm lad near Palmyra, New York," as he sometimes said.

The Bible, Human Reason, and Christian Experience

Conner emphasized always the element of human reason in the creation of the Bible and its use. He began his discussions of Christian doctrine by listing three ingredients that he considered necessary for any legitimate theological system that calls itself Christian: (1) The Bible, (2) human reason, and (3) Christian experience.

Conner spoke with derision of those who thought the Bible could confront a human being as revelatory apart from the exercise of man's reason. Because it bears directly on this matter and echoes so thoroughly his classroom discussions of this topic, I am going to quote a large segment of a journal he kept, intermittently, for a number of years.[6]

> Of course one would have to admit that man's reason cannot apprehend the idea of God and his dealings with man. We can start in any direction, in science, philosophy or religion, and we are soon up against mystery. But that is a different matter from asking me to accept as true a doctrine that is inherently measurable as immoral, simply on the ground that it is taught in the Scriptures. To ask men to quit thinking or stifle the voice of conscience while the preacher rams down their throats certain "revealed" truths is to ask the impossible. Some men do that for awhile. Some are doing it now. I heard Professor Rauschenbusch say (in a class in Church History) that many a man had crucified his intellect for God's sake. I did not understand at the time what he meant. Now I think I do.

6. W. T. Conner, "Here and There." The typescript which Conner had prepared, in its original form, is on file in the library of Southeastern Baptist Theological Seminary library, Wake Forest, North Carolina. I made use of this journal in my biography, *W. T. Conner: Theologian of the Southwest* (Nashville: Broadman Press, 1964), for example, on pp. 70, 71, 94, 99, 100.

While some men may do this for a while, in the end reason and conscience will assert themselves against any authority that seeks to suppress them. Why? Because they must. It is in their nature to do so. They cannot permanently be suppressed. God himself is immanent in the reason and conscience of man, and the motive power of the universe is surging up in them to accomplish its eternal purpose.

I used to hear another great teacher, Calvin Goodspeed [who briefly preceded Conner as professor of theology], say: "I am more certain that my mind comes from God than I am that any book comes from God." When I thought about his statement I saw that it was bound to be true. Suppose a book comes to me claiming to come from God. Shall I accept it just because it makes such a claim? Then I shall have to accept the *Koran,* Joseph Smith's *Book of Mormon,* Mrs. Eddy's *Science and Health.* Here they come making just such a claim. What shall I do? Test them, of course. Apply the test of historical and literary criticism, the test of inherent reasonableness. I shall see if their teachings square with the dictates of reason and conscience. Whatever comes to contradict sound reason and an enlightened conscience, I will reject, whether that means all or a part of their contents. I will not argue that I must accept all or none—I cannot honestly accept what is fundamentally contradictory or what is immoral in teaching.

If I apply these tests to these books, why not to the Bible? Why should I demand that these books square with the dictates of reason and conscience and then accept what is in the Bible, whether it is reasonable or not? The simple truth is that I cannot. The Bible must meet the dictates of reason and conscience. In one sense the Bible judges me. But I must also judge the Bible and I cannot accept it unless it stands the test of rational and moral judgment. And I cannot surrender the right to apply this test to any part of the Bible or any doctrine found in it.[7]

Often, when trying to enlarge upon the students' simple and mechanical concepts of biblical revelation, Conner would resort to a statement for which he became famous. "The Bible

7. "Here and There," 21–23.

does not always mean what it says but it always means what it means."

On one occasion, when engaged in an oral examination, he asked a student to translate a portion of one of Paul's epistles. Conner abruptly interrupted him to ask what connection the clause he had just read had with the rest of Paul's statement. The student hesitated as if reluctant to criticize Paul's grammar. Conner spoke, insisting that the clause had no connection with the rest of the statement. "Paul just started to say something and stopped in the middle of his sentence and went on to something else," he said.

An Open-minded, Conservative Scholar

On a similar occasion he asked a student which he would prefer, if stranded on a desert island, *Pilgrim's Progress* or the book of Leviticus. When the student said *Pilgrim's Progress* Conner rejoined: "Sure, it would be like asking whether one would prefer to have a live dog or his wife's right arm. Remember," he added, "there are some things that are more biblical than the Bible itself."

Conner should be classified, not as a liberal but as an open-minded conservative scholar. He often had occasion to pay his respects to those who were radical conservatives, whom he called "orthodox." In his journal he inscribed this remark, obviously made during the darkest days of the depression of the 1930s:

> Denominational plans may need changing. Baptist brag does not sound very good now. Much Baptist talk that I have heard sounds like Job's comforters. We are the people and wisdom will die with us. Dr. Carroll used to say that orthodoxy was making its last stand on Seminary Hill [that is, at Southwestern Seminary]. Two things might be remembered. One is that, after all, orthodoxy is not what the world needs.
>
> They tell us that orthodoxy is straight thinking. The orthodoxy that I have seen all my life was rather no thinking at all. It was an attitude of mind that accepted traditional doctrines and then the mind, lest it should depart from what was accepted,

committed suicide. Orthodoxy is an opiate to administer to young minds to guarantee that they will always be kept under control. Mind is a dangerous thing when it gets loose. It starts all kinds of uncomfortable things.

It interferes with the established interests.[8]

Some of the most controversial discussions in Conner's classes grew out of the mechanical, literalistic interpretation that students sometimes insisted on using in regard to biblical language. Normally he was patient with their contrary opinions and tolerantly set himself to analyzing their point of view. He did sometimes become exercised when one pressed his objections to the point of appearing to deny Conner the privilege of holding a contrary view. One such instance grew out of a discussion of whether the fires of hell were literal fire.

As far as I know this was the sole case in which Conner expelled a student from his class. Conner was advocating a point of view such as that expressed in his book, *The Gospel of Redemption*. "There are those who insist that the fire spoken of must be literal fire," he said in that place. "Moreover, to inflict purely physical pain on the sinner would not be to adapt his punishment to the nature of his sin. . . . Physical suffering would not be an adequate punishment for spiritual sins."[9]

I heard the encounter but have never been quite able to understand the student's terms of reaction. "You are a liar," he exclaimed, to which Conner promptly ushered him out of the room.

Enough has been said to indicate that those who knew him best knew Conner to be a soundly biblical theologian. Fundamentalists do not believe in the Book more sincerely, nor are they any more zealous in establishing their doctrinal ideas more firmly upon it than he. The crux of his judgment upon

8. Ibid., 9, 10.
9. W. T. Conner, *The Gospel of Redemption* (Nashville: Broadman Press, 1945), 351.

fundamentalism as a movement lay in his serious questions about the ultraconservative's conception of biblical authority, the cutting edge of where the Bible meets human experience. His criticism was summed up in his use of the distinction between what he called "identifying the substance with the form" of the scriptural teachings.

This is a mistake often made by people who insist on a literal interpretation and application of all biblical teachings. Speaking of such an approach he said:

> Such a program leads to all kinds of absurdities. It causes one to regard the Scriptures as a book of rules to which one can go to find specific directions for every situation that may arise. The Bible is not a book of rules of that kind. . . . What we need to do is to find the permanent truth and animating principles manifested in the Scriptures and apply that truth in a Christian spirit to our situation.

> This same error . . . has been the foundation of an argument against the religious validity of the Bible. For instance, it has been argued that the biblical writers had a certain world view. They regarded the world as having been created only a few thousand years ago. For them the world was the center of the universe and the sun, moon, and stars travelled around the earth. Man also was regarded as the center of interest for God and the whole of creation. The modern scientific view has changed all that. We now know that the world has been here a long, long, time, that man has been on the earth much longer than once supposed, that the sun is the center of our system and that out beyond this system are hundreds or thousands of others much larger than ours.

> The change that has taken place is a change in scientific views and does not affect the religious validity of the Bible.[10]

Conner resented the taunts of the Roman church to the effect that in the Reformation an infallible book was substituted for an infallible church. He thought they missed the whole point of Luther and others. It was not simply an

10. W. T. Conner, *Revelation and God* (Nashville: Broadman Press, 1936), 86–89.

exchange of authorities that occurred. The entire focus of authority was changed, he contended. The authority of church is oppressive. It presses its demands externally upon a person.

Moreover, the authority of an infallible book or an infallible creed makes the same mistake. The Bible is often represented as a book of statutes of that nature. It is not that kind of book. For a free moral being there can be no such authority. There is no authority that can dictate our decisions and actions. There is no authority for man that gives him an offhand solution for all moral and spiritual problems. We as individuals are obligated to seek to know the truth and we must strive to do it.

Conner: The Bible Is Preeminently a Book of Religion

God is a God of authority and biblical revelation is also authoritative; but both God and biblical revelation are the kind of authority that elicits, expects, and encourages human beings to become what they can become, by God's help. This means that for Conner the Bible is preeminently a book of religion. It does not claim to be authoritative in the realm of science, or mathematics, or history, or geography. That its interest was in conveying religious truth meant that it was couched in the limited experience of those to whom its truths came. It was not deterred by such limitations in conveying its religious truths. Its message was, therefore, a part of an ongoing, progressive revelation, the gradual but definite unfolding of knowledge of the religious character of the universe.[11]

In what appears to be a resort of desperation to acquire the good name of Conner as an advocate of their cause, the writers I have in mind refer to one sentence of his writings. By means of that sentence, they seek to associate him with all the ideas of Benjamin Warfield, a theologian renowned for his strict Calvinism. Conner agreed with Warfield, and with

11. Cf. *Revelation and God*, 97.

all others who believe in the Bible as inspired. In his *Revelation and God* he declared:

> The Bible is an inspired book. This we have specifically in the New Testament for the Old. Jesus so regarded it. . . . So did Paul. Paul says that "all Scripture is given by inspiration of God." Doctor Warfield is probably correct when he says that this means that God produced or caused the Scriptures.[12]

For both men this was a broad affirmation of divine inspiration about which there was never any question in Conner's thought. However, it would be a sorry piece of logic to conclude that, because Conner agreed with Warfield about inspiration, it follows that Conner agreed with him about any or all of Warfield's other ideas. This would suggest that, if Conner agreed with Warfield that the Bible is inspired, then it follows that if Warfield liked potato pancakes, Conner must have liked potato pancakes also.

From the sounds I hear coming from the camp of those who wish to claim W. T. Conner in this fashion, they have a strong ally for their biblical ideas in one who lived and worked in Fort Worth during the time Conner lived there. His name was not Conner. It was J. Frank Norris. Norris invested heavily in sowing the same kind of fundamentalist seed of prejudice and discord; and the harvest of his sowing these individuals are reaping very effectively.

*

12. Ibid., 84. The last sentence was quoted in Bush and Nettles, *Baptists and the Bible*, 320. It is apparently the basis for Draper's error that Conner agreed with Warfield and was thus an inerrantist. See the introduction to this chapter.

PART FOUR

THE BIBLE AND CONFESSIONS OF FAITH

What Kind of Protestants Are Baptists?

10

Creedalism, Confessionalism, and the Baptist Faith and Message

THOMAS J. NETTLES

Editor's Introduction

Baptists have been more consistent than most other Protestant groups in championing the Reformation principle of *sola scriptura*. That principle requires that the final authority for faith and practice shall be "Scripture alone": No creed, confession, church tradition, or church authority may compete with the Bible for that preeminence.[1]

Baptists and Confessions: John Leland

Of course, this "no creed but the Bible" theme has not been equally emphasized by all Baptists. And that fact provides the context for understanding one feature of Thomas Nettles' gentlemanly, hard-hitting chapter: He has selected Baptists of the more creedally inclined sort for treatment.

So far as the noncreedal inclinations of Southern Baptists are concerned, the most important tradition which Nettles fails to mention is that of the Separate Baptists. These fiery, independent, evangelistic people spilled over from the Great Awakening in New England and appeared in the South beginning in 1755. Their role in shaping the outlook of Southern Baptists has been enormous. And one of their most pronounced characteristics was their sharp antipathy toward confessions of faith.[2]

---

1. See Jaroslav Pelikan, *Reformation of Church and Dogma (1300–1700)*, *The Christian Tradition: A History of the Development of Doctrine*, vol. 4 (Chicago: University of Chicago Press, 1984), 341, 347; cf. pp. 264, 265.

2. Walter B. Shurden, "The Southern Baptist Synthesis," *Baptist History and Heritage*, 16 (April 1981), 4–6.

A classic statement on this point was penned in 1790 by the great Separate Baptist, John Leland, then of Virginia. It is quoted below. His statement appeals for freedom to pursue truth; but in a prior and more basic sense, his statement affirms *the sole authority of the Bible.* It speaks on behalf of the person who "believes the Bible with all his heart," and who therefore must be free—in order to be able to follow Scripture where it leads. No "system of religion," as Leland expresses it, should come between the soul and the Scriptures. For only as the soul is free from the dictates of any intervening system, and related *directly and freely* to the Bible, can the soul submit fully to the authority of Scripture.[3]

Here is the statement in which Leland expressed his reservations about having a confession of faith:

Why this Virgin Mary between the souls of men and the scriptures? Had a system of religion been essential to salvation, or even to the happiness of the saints, would not Jesus, who was faithful in all his house, have left us one? If he has, it is accessible to all [i.e., clearly stated in the Bible]. If he has not, why should a man be called a heretick because he cannot believe what he cannot believe, though he believes the Bible with all his heart? Confessions of faith often check any further pursuit after truth, confine the mind into a particular way of reasoning, and give rise to frequent separations. . . . It is sometimes said that hereticks are always averse to confessions of faith. I wish I could say as much of tyrants. But after all, if a confession of faith, upon the whole, may be advantageous, the greatest care should be taken not to *sacradize,* or make a petty Bible of it.[4]

Protestant Breakthrough

Leland's way of relating Christian freedom to the sole authority of the Bible was given confessional embodiment in 1925 when Southern Baptists adopted their first denominational statement of faith, the Baptist Faith and Message. An anticreedal

---

3. Leland's insistence upon being directly related to the Bible, unencumbered by any intervening "system of religion," makes him a clear and prepossessing advocate of the "simple biblicism" discussed in chapters 1 and 6.

4. John Leland, *The Writings of John Leland,* L. F. Greene, ed., (New York: Arno Press, 1969), 114.

preamble was built into the statement and the result is a break-through in the Protestant espousal of *sola scriptura.* Because of the way the preamble subordinates the ensuing confession of faith *to the Bible,* it provides a new kind of protection against the possibility that the confession might gain enough status to usurp the authority of the Bible itself.

For their first eighty years, Southern Baptists had been true to the statement issued by the founders of their convention in 1845: "We have constructed for our basis no new creed; acting in this matter upon a Baptist aversion for all creeds but the Bible."[5]

Objections to having a confession of faith were strong in 1925. These objections were met and overcome only by the strategy of a group which, "while not agreed on the necessity for a confession in the first place, . . . were willing to have a confession as long as its authority was carefully limited and its scope restricted to religious matters."[6]

This "limitation of scope" and "restriction of authority" were achieved most definitively in a clearly marked-off section of the preamble which I shall call the "nature and function" section. The section in question is made up of five tightly-worded paragraphs.[7] The paragraphs verbatim the same in the 1925 and the 1963 Faith and Message, set forth "the historic Baptist conception of the nature and function of confessions of faith in our religious and denominational life."[8] Since the confession of faith which follows the preamble is a confession in Baptist life, the five paragraphs govern it: They define and delimit its status and authority, its "nature and function."

In the words of the chairman of the 1963 drafting committee, Herschel Hobbs, "Without [the preamble] the statement becomes a creed. And Baptists are not a creedal people. With-

5. Robert A. Baker, ed., *A Baptist Source Book* (Nashville: Broadman, 1966), 120.

6. Walter B. Shurden, "Southern Baptist Responses to Their Confessional Statements," *Review and Expositor* 76 (Winter 1979), 75.

7. The five paragraphs appear, in their entirety, on pp. 158, 159 of this book.

8. I quote from the Baptist Faith and Message here and hereafter from *Annual* of the *SBC, 1963* (Nashville: Executive Committee of the SBC, 1963), 269–281, where the 1925 and 1963 texts appear side by side.

out this preamble the convention would not have adopted it."[9]

I want to explain the freshness of the Baptist Faith and Message by commenting on both of the points, freedom and authority, which are involved in its preamble. Nettles also addresses the two points, partly in response to an article of mine.[10]

Freedom: Consensus Statements

Paragraph 1 of the "nature and function" section of the Faith and Message says Baptist confessions of faith "constitute a consensus of opinion of some Baptist body."

What does that mean if more than one "opinion" on some doctrine is importantly represented within a "Baptist body"? It means that a confessional statement, if it addresses that doctrine, must have "breadth."[11] It must have "affirmative ambiguity," as it might be called (to distinguish it from the ambiguity of indifference or inattention). It must express the doctrine in such a way as to leave open the alternative ways of believing that doctrine which are importantly represented in that body of Baptists. If that kind of affirmative ambiguity is missing or removed, the result is simply not a Baptist confession of faith.

A notable example of this kind of ambiguity is the statement in Article I of the Faith and Message, that the Bible "has . . . truth, without any mixture of error, for its matter." Along with coauthor Russ Bush, Nettles stated in 1980 that the statement "does not exclude either group of interpreters from affirming the confessional statement," neither strict inerrantists, nor those for whom the Bible's contents require a different view.[12]

Nettles returns to the point in this chapter, and expresses interest in removing that ambiguity. But if that is done, consider

---

9. Herschel H. Hobbs, "Southern Baptists and Confessionalism: A Comparison of the Origins and Contents of the 1925 and 1963 Confessions," *Review and Expositor* 76 (Winter 1979), 68.

10. Robison B. James, "BFM Statement: Best Answer," *SBC Today*, 4 (October 1986), 8, 9.

11. Hobbs reports approvingly the comment of one member of his 1963 drafting committee that, though a certain formulation would have expressed that person's view well, he did not want it in the statement they were drafting: the statement "must be broad enough for all of them to live comfortably with it." Hobbs, "Southern Baptists and Confessionalism," 60.

12. L. Russ Bush and Tom J. Nettles, *Baptists and the Bible* (Chicago: Moody Press, 1980), pp. 390, 391.

the result: either (a) the confession would no longer be a Baptist confession or (b) it would be a consensus statement all right, but a consensus statement of a *smaller* body of Baptists than the body which previously gave its free consent to the confession.

Sole Authority

The Faith and Message states a strong view of *sola scriptura* in paragraph 4 of its "nature and function" section. That paragraph, in its entirety, says "That the sole authority for faith and practice among Baptists is the Scriptures of the Old and New Testaments. Confessions are only guides in interpretation, having no authority over the conscience."

If we take this "Scripture only" principle seriously, it forces us to be jealous for the authority of the Bible, lest our own ways of construing it prevail over the nature and contents of the Bible itself. A systematic inerrancy theory, at least when it is legislated for others in a confessional statement, turns this upside down.

Instead of allowing the faithful to submit directly to the authority of what confronts them in Scripture *on the Bible's own terms,* strict confessionalized inerrancy requires, in an absolute and a priori way, that the Bible must be read and interpreted in conformity with the inerrantist preconception—notwithstanding anything the Bible might say or indicate to the contrary. On the points it touches, the inerrancy preconception is clearly superior to the status of the Bible's unfolding deliverances themselves.

The Bible is recognized as God's Word, yes. But God is in fact allowed no choice, no alternative, no matter how he has given his Word nor how he wills to speak through it. (For example, God is precluded from *effectively* issuing a priority, overriding claim on us, a point I explain in chapter 6.)[13]

Allowing God's Word the freedom to be authoritative in its own way does not force us to affirm errors. It rather leaves God free from *our human notions of what errors are,* notions that we would otherwise impose upon him and his Word at every turn.[14]

13. See pp. 79–82, including note 16.
14. To their credit, honest inerrantists work hard to head off the misunderstandings of the Bible which the notion of inerrancy invites people to fall into. One way they do this is by spelling out numerous "exceptions" or "qualifications" to what they *mean* when they say the Bible is without error (the nine in the Chicago Statement, Art. 13, are a short list). What

Nettles' point in this chapter is well taken that we should not say the Baptist Faith and Message, or any confession, is divinely inspired. It is not the divine *sufficiency* of that confession that makes many Southern Baptists want to stick loyally by it without embellishing it. It is rather the fact that it makes its own *insufficiency* clear. By virtue of its preamble-confession structure, it holds itself in check in a way no known alternative does. It steadfastly refuses to encroach either upon the Bible's rightful authority or the Christian's proper liberty. In Leland's colorful terms, the Baptist Faith and Message reins itself in from being either a "petty Bible" or a "system of religion" between the soul and the Scriptures.

Much consternation currently exists concerning the relationship between confessions, creeds, and the authority of Scripture. While this chapter will probably not clear the air on this issue, the author intends to address some of the pivotal entanglements involved in the intertwining of Scripture with the human attempts to understand it. This is something of an "It seems to me" presentation which, I hope, will bring at least as much light as heat to the discussion.

First, all Christians[1] affirm that God alone is wise. He only is eternal, immortal, and in his essence truth itself. All he speaks is true, and he alone knows all the truth and knows it exhaustively. Any attempt, therefore, to affirm truth as having independent or contradictory existence to that which is known of God is irreverent. Acceptance of any authority above or alongside God's authority is idolatrous.

Second, all Christians agree that God is a revealing God. While he is finally incomprehensible (none can put boundaries around him), unknowable, and unsearchable, he

---

this says is that, in the sense ordinary people use the word, the Bible is *not* free of "error." Rather, it is errorless in a special sense they would not be likely to think of, a sense they have a hard time keeping straight.

1. This assertion is admittedly bold because of the ironical state of Christian theology today. Whether Process Theology can fly under the banner of Christianity may be a subject of debate.

can be known truthfully though not exhaustively through faculties which he has incorporated within our natures as points of contact with him: that is, our minds, wills, affections, and consciences. We can know him savingly, therefore, and we can know enough of his character to evoke a constant crescendo of praise, worship, and adoration.

Third, all Christians accept Scripture as, at least, a part of a fabric of revelatory material upon which salvation and worship is known and defined. Most Christians accept Scripture as the major factor in their knowledge of God. Roman Catholicism has placed some degree of authority in "unwritten tradition," which from time to time takes the form of dogma through a declaration of the magisterium of the church under a claimed guidance of the Holy Spirit. Quakerism placed personal experience and the "inner light" on a level essentially superior to what they considered the "dead letter" of Scripture.[2]

Baptists have stressed the Reformation principle of *sola scriptura*, that is, Scripture alone is the foundation of our knowledge of God and the depository (2 Timothy 1:12-14) of divine truth. This has been so often and so thoroughly enunciated, and in such decisive and emphatic terms, that it would seem none could disavow the principle, at least from a historical perspective. Other realities such as experience, reason, and confession have served as aids in understanding but not in the full sense of an "authority." All concerned parties in the current crisis must be careful not to place any other entity, whether existential or written, above Scripture. Neither catechism, creed, or confession—nor reason, conscience, or current experience should be allowed to eclipse a clear and plain Scripture affirmation at any time.

Given such a proper submission to biblical authority, how should one regard confessions of faith? All should readily

2. For some discussion of Baptist reaction to Quaker views of Scripture, see L. Russ Bush and Tom J. Nettles, *Baptists and the Bible* (Chicago: Moody Press, 1980), pp. 40-44, 56, 57, 78-80.

acknowledge, along with the Preamble of the Baptist Faith and Message, that confessions are only "guides in interpretation, having no authority over the conscience." They are useful, however, in several ways and have been advantageous in conserving the particulars of Baptist life. From the abundance of Baptist confessions in existence, the following principles have been condensed: (1) the constructive contribution of confessions, (2) their necessary changeableness, and (3) their relation to Scripture.

Constructive Contribution

1. *A human document.* That we acknowledge a confession as strictly a humanly composed document is an important step in a quest for unity. All conservative Christian denominations believe that their theologies and ecclesiologies are true reflections of biblical teaching. Hardly any sincere Christian would say, "You are biblical and obviously I am not, but I will stay what I am." Though they disagree, they both believe their position is biblical. The human document meets the essential need of revealing the different understandings of the Bible. When these understandings differ significantly in vital areas, unity of purpose and mission become difficult if not impossible.

For this reason, the scheme of Thomas Campbell and Alexander Campbell was impracticable. In 1809, Thomas Campbell set forth the ideal in his *Declaration and Address*, in which he called for a subduing of all inferential theology to a direct "Thus saith the Lord." Claiming admirably that "nothing ought to be inculcated upon Christians as articles of faith . . . but what is expressly taught and enjoined upon them in the word of God," he also insisted that "no such deduction or inferential truths ought to have any place in the Church's confession"; such confessional extrapolations Campbell called "stumbling-blocks—the rubbish of ages."[3]

3. Thomas Campbell, *Declaration and Address* (St. Louis: Mission Messenger, 1972), 45–49.

His son Alexander continued this call for freedom from confessions. This attitude led Robert B. Semple, of Virginia, to characterize Campbell's view as unbaptistic.

Some of your opinions, though true, are pushed to extremes, such as those upon the use of creeds, confessions, . . . In short your views are generally so contrary to those of Baptists in general, that if a party was to go fully into the practice of your principles I should say a new sect had sprung up, radically different from the Baptists, as they now are.[4]

When Baptist Associations began to disfellowship the followers of Campbell, one of his sentiments repugnant to those Associations was "That no creed is necessary for the Church, but the Scriptures as they stand."[5]

J. P. Boyce himself saw this danger in the ideas of Campbell and warned the trustees of Furman against a repeat of Campbell's error. "Playing upon the prejudices of the weak and ignorant among our people, decrying creeds as an infringement upon the rights of conscience, making a deep impression by his extensive learning and great abilities, Alexander Campbell threatened at one time the total destruction of our faith."[6] Boyce continued that Baptists had used creeds in two ways: to declare their own faith and to test its existence in others.[7]

A large part, therefore, of the constructive contribution of a confession lies precisely at the point of its being a human and interpretive document. The exegetical and annunciatory character of confessions makes them valuable for creating and testing the unity of Christians on the teachings of Scripture.

4. Robert A. Baker, ed., *A Baptist Source Book* (Nashville: Broadman Press, 1966), 78.

5. Ibid.

6. John A. Broadus, *Memoir of James P. Boyce* (New York: Armstrong and Son, 1893), 140.

7. J. P. Boyce, *Three Changes in Theological Institutions* (Greenville, S.C.: C. J. Elford's Book and Job Press, 1856), 41.

2. *Witness to the coherence of truth.* Confessions are possible and necessary as witnesses to a belief in the coherence of truth. Scriptural data related to any subject can be synthesized (obviously with proper attention to contextual interpretation) so as to produce a biblical doctrine.

The most obvious example of such a doctrine is that of the Trinity. With the mention of Father, Son, and Spirit as separate personal subsistences in Scripture and the clear monotheistic commitment of all the Bible—plus the ascription of the attributes of deity to each of the three Persons—one can do justice to the total biblical witness only by confession of the orthodox doctrine of the Trinity. This necessary synthesizing of biblical data is most thoroughly done under the power of a commitment to inerrancy (that is, the pervasive, coherent truthfulness of Scripture). This conviction, therefore, constitutes the clearest and most consistent foundation for a biblical confession of faith. Without such commitment, some part of a doctrine could be dismissed on the basis of a bias toward another authority.

The treatment of 1 Samuel 15:3 is a case in point. The command to utterly destroy Amalek, "man and woman, infant and suckling, ox and sheep, camel and ass" (RSV) is viewed by some as unworthy of the God and Father of our Lord Jesus Christ. This represents a clear case where no discrepancy about numbers, order of events, or textual variants clouds the discussion. The text is rejected as it is and forms no part of theology for that person. This part of Scripture loses its authority because it violates an independent standard held by the rejecter. Whether this standard arises from another place in Scripture, an autonomous ethical commitment, or a rationalistic assumption, it is clear that a commitment to the coherent truth of the entire corpus of Scripture is absent, and Holy Scripture is not the authority.

The admission of such a principle immediately renders nugatory the attempt to construct a biblical confession. The confession may represent the beliefs a person has as a result of familiarity with the *part* of the Bible that he or she has chosen to accept, for whatever reason; but it cannot be a confession in the historic sense that the confession expresses beliefs arising from an engagement with and submission to the authority of "all Scripture" (2 Timothy 3:16).

This very tendency in his own day led B. H. Carroll into a strong affirmation of the use of "creeds" and their purpose of reflecting the total of Scripture. In his comments on Ephesians 4:1–16, Carroll pointed out that a "Christian creed should enlarge, and not diminish, up to the last utterance of revelation in order that each article might be transmitted into experience." Each church should aim at the same goal, for "The more doctrines a church can agree on, the greater its power. . . . The fewer its articles of faith, the fewer its bonds of union and compactness." In fact, according to Carroll, "The longest creed of history is more valuable and less hurtful than the shortest."[8]

Carroll also spoke to the apparent tension between creed and liberty in uncompromising terms. "The modern cry, 'Less creed and more liberty,' is a degeneration from the vertebrate to the jellyfish," Carroll insisted; "and means less unity and less morality, and it means more heresy." After warning his reader against any who decried doctrines, Carroll continued, "We are entitled to no liberty in these matters. It is a positive and very hurtful sin to magnify liberty at the expense of doctrine."[9]

Carroll entertained no doubts or mental reservations about the veracity of any part of Scripture or its coherent relationship with all other parts. Thus his call for the enlarged and continually refined "creed."

3. *Commitment to unity.* Confessions represent a commitment to guarantee a faithful and conscientious unity. The Baptist Faith and Message affirms that "Confessions are only guides in interpretation, having no authority over the

8. B. H. Carroll, *An Interpretation of the English Bible* (Nashville: Broadman Press, 1948), 140, 147.
9. Ibid., 146, 147.

conscience." This is certainly as it should be. Baptists have, however, insisted that all who sign a confession do so conscientiously and make every effort to maintain the unity implicit in a confession of faith.

When General Baptists in England were rescued from destruction by a doctrinal reformation under the leadership of Dan Taylor in 1770, a confession of faith was adopted which required strict adherence from all ministers of their new connection. The preface to the confession stated:

> We agree, that no minister be permitted to join this assembly, who does not subscribe the articles we have now agreed upon; and that those who do subscribe, and afterwards depart from them, shall be considered as no longer belonging to this assembly.

The Philadelphia Association, the first Baptist Association in the United States, considered a conscientious acceptance of its confession a matter of grave importance. Answering a query concerning some doctrines of the confession, that is, the foreknowledge of God and its implications, the Association then set the matter of conscience and confessions in a startling light. The question was posed:

> Whether such a member of the church holding such an opinion endeavors to propagate it, and obstinately persists in it, is not worthy of the highest censure, notwithstanding he pleads matters of conscience?
>
> Answer. We judge such worthy of the highest censure; because a church is to proceed against a person who is erroneous in judgment, as well as one vicious in practice, notwithstanding they may plead conscience in the matter. Tit. iii 10; 2 Thess. iii 14.[10]

Is this a violation of the heritage of Roger Williams? Not at all. It is the proper application of a confession of faith which

---

10. *Minutes of the Philadelphia Association 1707–1807*, ed. A. D. Gillette (Philadelphia: American Baptist Publication Society, 1851), 58.

expresses the position of a voluntary body. J. P. Boyce presented this same viewpoint in his argument for the signing of an abstract of doctrine by seminary professors. Boyce argued, "No difference, however slight, no particular sentiment, however speculative, is here allowable." Furthermore, continued Boyce, "His agreement with the standard should be exact. His declaration of it should be based upon no mental reservation, upon no private understanding with those who immediately invest him into office."[11]

Boyce considered this no violation of conscience, for it inflicts no bodily punishment or civil disability in the church-state relation but is a protection of the spirituality of the church and simplicity that is in Christ. His encouragement of the trustees at Furman to require the adherence to an abstract of doctrine clearly foreshadowed his own intention for The Southern Baptist Theological Seminary.

> You will infringe the rights of no man, and you will secure the rights of those who have established here an instrumentality for the production of a sound ministry. It is no hardship to those who teach here, to be called upon to sign the declaration of their principles, for there are fields of usefulness open elsewhere to every man, and none need accept your call who cannot conscientiously sign your formulary.[12]

The same conviction was expressed by J. B. Gambrell when he was editor of the *Baptist Standard* in Texas. With equal intensity he declared both his willingness to fight for the protection of freedom of thought and speech as well as the rights of Baptists to insist on doctrinal purity in the pulpit and classroom. If a man departs from Baptist doctrine, Gambrell insisted that none should seek to "abridge his thinking, nor his defense of his thinking." But that man "passes the bounds of liberty" and indulges in "arrogant license" when he uses an institution and its resources to dilute or overthrow "the faith which the institution was founded to build up." Such a man

11. Boyce, *Three Changes*, 35.
12. Ibid., 44.

should "resign his place and exercise his liberty without infringing on the rights of others."[13]

Baptists have insisted on liberty of conscience within civil society in order that conscientious union with voluntary societies, such as the church, be possible. Confessions of faith have defined the framework of conscientious commitment for Baptists.

Changeableness of Confessions

The progression, digression, and regression of men's belief result in changed confessions. History is filled with men whose convictions and loyalties change either for the better or the worse. A look at the lives of John Smyth, Thomas Collier, Benjamin Keach, Abraham Booth, and a myriad of others demonstrates this.

Confessions change for other reasons, too. Historical challenges to the "faith once delivered to the saints" have brought to birth sometimes longer, sometimes shorter, sometimes more precise, and sometimes more ambiguous confessions. Each change came about from a perceived theological need.

The Creed of Nicea, 325, did no harm to the universally accepted rule of faith (now known as the Apostles' Creed) but strengthened its affirmation of the deity of Christ with at least four ingenious verbal additions to refute soundly the heresy of Arius. In like manner, the Tome of Leo, in 451, at Chalcedon, set forth a universally acceptable statement on the relation between the divine and human natures of Christ. Neither of the statements was received as superior to Scripture or out of harmony with the historic belief of the church. Both, however, captured the theological necessities of their age perfectly.

Baptists have been willing to clarify confessions when such revisions grow "out of present needs." They have affirmed strongly that "Baptists should hold themselves free to revise

---

13. J. B. Gambrell, *Ten Years in Texas* (Dallas: The Baptist Standard, 1910), 128, 129.

their statements of faith as may seem to them wise and expedient at any time."[14]

Because confessions normally are worded carefully and arise from intense deliberation and represent the considered, settled, and mature convictions of a large body of people who have saturated themselves with Scripture, as well as the questions and answers of past and current theological deliberations, alterations in a major confession should be pursued only under the pain of intense need. Sometimes confessions have noses of wax, purposefully to be bent this way or that if both bends are considered within biblically evangelical parameters. And, sometimes an ambiguity is discerned in the heat of later controversy which has the potential of being theologically destructive if left uncorrected. Such was the case with the confession of Eusebuis at the Council of Nicea. Everything it affirmed was right, but it left enough unsaid that Arius himself could sign it. Enter, therefore, Athanasius. Stability and alterability must characterize a confession and a people's attitude toward it.

Three attitudes toward confessions indicate an unhealthy view of them. The first, already discussed, consists of a refusal to give legitimate conscientious affirmation to it in its proper sphere of influence. The second consists of imputing immutability to its phrases and words; the result of this is that it can become static and not dynamically related to vital theological concerns.[15] The third consists of conceding the presence of extraordinary divine activity and guidance in the production of a confession so as to attribute to it the characteristics of inspiration. Claims of providence in the production of the 1963 Baptist Faith and Message so as to render alteration impious, unfaithful, divisive, and pharisaical have appeared in our day. These represent lamentable

14. *Annual of the SBC, 1925*, 71.
15. The time may soon come when the theological issues raised by Liberation Theology and Process Theology will call for special treatment in the Baptist Faith and Message.

lapses into an ironical creedalism and give to the confession a place that should be reserved for Scripture.

Confessions and Scripture

Changes should be considered in a confession only when an issue is deemed of sufficient importance to merit the attention. And then the change might be accompanied by an addendum instead of a textual alteration.

Since the entire purpose of a confession is to give as accurate a reflection as possible of full scriptural teaching on a subject, the doctrine of Scripture looms as an extremely important area for clear affirmation. It is self-contradictory for a confession's position on Scripture to allow a belief that the Bible corrects (and thus contradicts) itself; that current human gifts and scholarship are so advanced that we unerringly discern discrepancies in Scripture; or that humility of mind consists of conceding variant accounts in Scripture to be irreconcilable. For a confession to lead to those positions, either in purpose or result, is intolerable. Instead, a confession's statement on Scripture should be so strong and clear that no hint of freedom to modify, omit, or reject the clear teaching of a text exists.

The phrase "without mixture of error" in the Baptist Faith and Message appears to fulfill the above expectations. The last phrase reads, "The criterion by which the Bible is to be interpreted is Jesus Christ." Historically, this would mean that Christ is the fulfillment of all Old Testament types and ceremonies. He is the complete revelation. Practically, some take this to mean that Christ in his word and work at times contradicts and corrects other portions of Holy Scripture. Is it possible for our perception of the Spirit of Christ to serve as an independent canon of criticism for the rest of Scripture? This author would say no, for we never find any words or actions of Jesus to justify it. Jesus set his interpretation and authority above that of the Pharisees and their traditions, but never in contradiction to his Scripture, our Old Testament.

If the wording of the Baptist Faith and Message permits agreement with the confession and a concurrent disagreement with the Scripture, then, just like the Athanasian correction of the Eusebian Creed, unequivocal clarification is needed. To do less exalts the confession above the Scripture and gives it independent and idolatrous authority.

Unswerving belief of Scripture does not remove God from the center of the church's worship; it exalts him by encouraging unreserved trust in his work as faithful, impeccable revealer as well as sure redeemer. The doctrine of inerrancy does not encourage an arrogant self-assuredness; it requires a humble submission of reason, affection, will, and conscience to the self-disclosure of God. Full acceptance of *pasa graphe* (each and every Scripture) does not open an escape from the rough road of careful interpretation; it obligates the interpreter to deal, not only with the easy, comforting parts of the Bible, but with the tough and heart-wrenching also. The Christian should never view acceptance of the full truthfulness of the biblical text as an unbearable yoke; it is, instead, the light that shines in a dark place until the Lord himself shows us his personal glory (2 Pet. 1:19).

11

Biblical Authority in Baptist Confessions of Faith, 1610–1963

WILLIAM R. ESTEP, JR.

Editor's Introduction

There is almost a plot, as it were, to the true story which William Estep tells in this chapter. He states it succinctly in the fifth paragraph of his essay.

In telling this story well, Estep's chapter assumes an honored place alongside other studies of the way Baptists have expressed their loyalty to the Bible in their confessions of faith.

One other study that is especially pertinent to the subject of this book is a compact article of 1979 by Estep's colleague at Southwestern Seminary, Professor James Leo Garrett, Jr.[1] In his article, Garrett makes the following two points, among others:

1. "One must come to the twentieth century before one finds in Baptist confessions of faith an application of the term 'infallible' to the inspiration of the Bible. Such an application is found exclusively in Landmark and Fundamentalist confessions."[2]

2. By contrast with such views, Baptists' historic confessions normally attribute a *functional* infallibility to the Bible in its "role as the supreme rule of faith, conduct, and worship. . . ."[3] As The Second London and Philadelphia Confessions say, the Bible "is the only sufficient, certain, and infallible *rule* of all *saving* Knowledge, Faith and Obedience" (emphasis added).

1. James L. Garrett, Jr., "Biblical Authority According to Baptist Confessions of Faith," *Review & Expositor*, 76 (Winter 1979), 43–54.
2. Ibid., 47.
3. Ibid., 48.

There is considerable confusion today regarding biblical authority. This confusion is evident in the suggestion that what is needed is a new creed or confession of faith that would constitute a rule of faith, demanding adherence to "essential doctrines," prominent among which is the concept of the inerrancy of Scripture. Apparently quite a few church people, including many Southern Baptists, feel the need of "nailing down" a concept of religious authority that cannot be challenged or evaded.

The expressed desire in this quest for an ultimate religious authority must be taken seriously. As P. T. Forsyth wrote, "The intellectual, and especially the moral situation of the age raises with ever growing force what I have called the central question of religion, and therefore of everything—the question as to authority."[1] It is not surprising then that the inerrancy controversy has produced such shock waves among Baptists and others because it is concerned with religious authority.

This is not true among Roman Catholics, since the locus of authority for them lies within the papacy. Nor is it true of some other communions, whose source of religious authority lies outside the biblical revelation. That the Bible is authoritative for Baptists is a general assumption difficult to refute.

The nature and use of that authority can best be understood, however, by examining certain influential confessions of faith in their historical contexts. Among the conclusions of such an examination, explained below, are the following.

Until 1677, Baptist confessions began with articles on God. Commencing with The Second London Confession of 1677 and 1688, however, major Baptist confessions gave first place to the Bible. That order was taken over directly from The Westminster Confession of 1646, a Presbyterian statement. The early Baptist pattern of giving priority of place to God and

---

1. P. T. Forsyth, *The Principle of Authority* (London: Independent Press, Ltd., 1952), 17.

Jesus Christ never completely disappeared. In the 1925 and 1963 revisions of The New Hampshire Confession, called The Baptist Faith and Message, Southern Baptists attempted to recover much of the original Baptist confessional emphasis. The preamble of The Baptist Faith and Message becomes particularly significant in reinforcing this impression.

The Role of Confessions

Baptists are not a creedal but a confessional people. The fundamental differences between creeds and confessions should not be ignored. Creeds are authoritative and often viewed as final and unalterable statements of faith. They are also sometimes viewed as infallible. As Schaff has stated, "The Greek Church confines the claim of infallibility to the seven oecumenical councils, from the first Council of Nicaea, 325, to the second of Nicaea, 787." He continues, "The Roman Church extends the same claim to the Council of Trent and all the subsequent official Papal decisions on questions of faith. . . ."[2] Frequently these creeds, including the Augsburg Confession (1530), anathematized those who held contrary opinions.

On the other hand, Baptists have never claimed ultimate authority for their confessions. These confessions, from 1610 to 1963, regardless of the circumstances that called them into existence, acknowledged the sufficiency of biblical authority for the faith and order of the churches (although that issue was not always explicitly addressed).

Baptist confessions are by no means uniform. The variety of emphases reflect both the understanding of faith of the group framing the confession and the historical situation that called it forth. Therefore, confessions are often uneven and incomplete expressions of the Christian faith. The nature of a particular confession was largely dependent upon the purpose for which it was formulated at the time. Robert G.

2. Philip Schaff, *The Creeds of Christendom*, Vol. I (Grand Rapids, Michigan: Baker Book House, 1877), 8.

Torbet has summarized five uses of Baptist confessions of faith as follows:

> (1) to maintain purity of doctrine; (2) to clarify and validate the Baptist position; (3) to serve as a guide to the General Assembly or local association in counselling churches; (4) to serve as a basis for fellowship within local churches, associations, or a General Assembly; (5) to discipline churches and members.[3]

Torbet's second use, "to clarify and validate the Baptist position," does not adequately state the most common purpose of seventeenth-century Baptist confessions, English and American, which was to publish before the world a true and correct summary of Baptist faith and practice.

One of the clearest statements regarding the "nature and function" of Baptist confessions of faith was published by the Southern Baptist Convention in 1925. This statement cleared the way for Southern Baptists' first confession of faith and virtually eliminated any opposition from those who had previously rejected any confessional statement on grounds of principle.

In 1963, the committee that revised the 1925 Faith and Message retained this five-point statement as part of the preamble to the revised confession. The statement, discussed in the editor's introduction to the preceding chapter, describes the purpose and limits of Baptist confessional statements. In their entirety, the five paragraphs of the statement read as follows:

> (1) That they [confessions] constitute a consensus of opinion of some Baptist body, large or small, for the general instruction and guidance of our own people and others concerning those articles of the Christian faith which are most surely held among us. They are not intended to add anything to the simple conditions of salvation revealed in the New Testament, viz., repentance towards God and faith in Jesus Christ as Saviour and Lord.

3. Robert G. Torbet, *A History of the Baptists* (Valley Forge: Judson Press, 1950), 46.

(2) That we do not regard them as complete statements of our faith, having any quality of finality or infallibility. As in the past so in the future Baptists should hold themselves free to revise their statements of faith as may seem to them wise and expedient at any time.

(3) That any group of Baptists, large or small, have the inherent right to draw up for themselves and publish to the world a confession of their faith whenever they may think it advisable to do so.

(4) That the sole authority for faith and practice among Baptists is the Scriptures of the Old and New Testaments. Confessions are only guides in interpretation, having no authority over the conscience.

(5) That they are statements of religious convictions, drawn from the Scriptures, and are not to be used to hamper freedom of thought or investigation in other realms of life.[4]

Antecedents

Baptists did not invent confessions. The Reformation stimulated a new era in the formulation of Protestant doctrinal statements. They were designed to set forth the major lines of demarcation distinguishing the communion issuing the confession from the Roman church, and from other Protestants as well. The most important of these were The Augsburg Confession (1530) and The Apology of The Augsburg Confession (1530) of the Lutherans, and the First and Second Helvetic Confessions, 1536 and 1566, respectively, of the Swiss Reformed Church.

The immediate antecedents of the first Baptist confessions, however, were (1) a Mennonite confession entitled A Brief Confession of the Principal Articles of the Christian Faith drawn up by Hans de Ries and Lubbert Gerrits in 1580, and (2) A True Confession of English Separatists living in Amsterdam in 1596. These two confessions represent

---

4. *Annual of the SBC, 1925,* 71. The revised and enlarged confession follows the preamble on pp. 71–76. The committee which drew up the 1925 statement was composed of S. M. Brown, W. J. McGlothlin, E. C. Dargan, L. R. Scarborough, and E. Y. Mullins, chairman.

divergent streams, Anabaptist and Calvinist, respectively, which are reflected in varying degrees in the emergence of the two major seventeenth-century Baptist movements. The Mennonite confession became the inspiration and model for the early General Baptist confessions prepared by John Smyth and Thomas Helwys (1610–1612), and A True Confession became the model for the first Particular Baptist confession (1644).

The Bible in General Baptist Confessions

So far as their history can be documented, Baptists appear to have arisen in the early seventeenth century out of an English-Puritan-Separatist milieu, under the influence of continental Anabaptism. John Smyth, a Puritan minister of the Church of England, separated from the church and formed a Separatist congregation at Gainesborough. While in exile in Amsterdam, he inaugurated baptism upon one's profession of faith by baptizing himself.

Subsequently, Smyth sought to unite with the Dutch Waterland Mennonite Church, an Anabaptist congregation. At this point, Thomas Helwys, the most prominent layman of the group, forsook Smyth and the majority. Taking about nine or ten others with him, he formed his own congregation, which returned to England in 1612.

During the five years or so Helwys was in the Netherlands, confessions of faith were exchanged with the Mennonites by both congregations. From these confessions and the accompanying correspondence, we learn something of the role of the Bible, its authority, and interpretation, which helped give birth to the English Baptist movement.

These earliest Baptists became known as General Baptists, since they held to a "general atonement," or the belief that Christ died for all men, not just for the elect. Not all their confessions were of equal importance, but taken together they constitute a family of confessions, the influence of which may be seen today. Our concern here is the role of Scripture in these confessions from 1610–1660.

The first confession drawn up by John Smyth (1609–10) was sent to the Waterland Mennonites when he asked them to accept the English into their church. It did not accomplish its purpose. A second confession of faith, an abbreviated form of The Waterland Confession of 1580, came from the Smyth congregation in 1610. The numerous scriptural references found in the Mennonite confession were omitted, and no one article was devoted to the Bible, but a number of articles reflect that the Smyth-led church looked to the Scriptures for instruction and doctrine.

The first article, although devoted to affirming their faith in God, begins, "We believe, through the power and instruction of the Holy Scriptures that there is one only God, . . ." The second article follows in a similar fashion: "2. This only God in the Holy Scriptures is manifested and revealed in Father, Son and Holy Ghost, being three, and nevertheless but one God" (102–103).[5]

As in the earlier Waterland Confession, Old and New Testaments are juxtaposed. Referring to Christ, article 10 declares: "In him is fulfilled, and by him is taken away, an intolerable burden of the law of Moses, . . ." (105). Article 11 then speaks of "the true promised Prophet" who "hath manifested and revealed unto us whatsoever God asketh or requireth of the people of the New Testament" as "God, by Moses and the other prophets, hath spoken and declared his will to the people of the Old Testament . . ." (105). Forty-two signatures of the English congregation, with that of Smyth heading the list, testify to an acceptance of this confession.

By 1611, Helwys, who had studied law and who up to this time had been a stalwart supporter of Smyth, parted company with his pastor. He insisted that Smyth's self-baptism —the means whereby Smyth had inaugurated baptism upon one's profession of faith—was valid, as was his subsequent

5. This citation, and subsequent parenthesized numbers within the text, refer to pages from William L. Lumpkin, *Baptist Confessions of Faith* (Philadelphia: Judson Press, 1959).

baptism of his entire church. He also insisted upon the autonomy of the local church and its right to "administer in all the holy ordinances, although as yet they have no Officers, or that their Officers should bee in Prison, sick, or by anie other meanes hindered from the Church" (120). Therefore, he rejected Smyth and the majority who had petitioned the Mennonites for membership.

In order to establish the identity of his own small group as distinct from that of the Mennonites, Helwys, with the help of his congregation, drew up what has been called "the first English Baptist Confession of Faith." While, as Lumpkin points out, it shows considerable independence of thought, it also reflects Mennonite influence as well as dependence upon the writings of John Smyth.

The Helwys confession, like that of Mennonites and like A True Confession, cites numerous Scripture references to support its twenty-seven articles. The arrangement of the articles follows the pattern set by the Mennonite confession. The confession begins with a discussion of the nature of God. Six additional articles are devoted to the functions of Christ as prophet, priest, and king. Article 23 sets forth the Helwys congregation's view of Scripture.

> That the scriptures off the Old and New Testament are written for our instruction, 2. Tim. 3.16 & that wee ought to search them for they testifie off CHRIST, Io. 5.39. And therefore to bee vsed withall reverence, as conteyning the Holie Word off GOD, which onelie is our direction in all thinges whatsoever. (122)

Apparently the phrase "Holie Word off God" used here refers to the kerygma, or gospel of Christ. The ninth article makes it clear that Helwys held to the finality of Jesus Christ to whom the Scriptures bear witness.

> That IESVS CHRIST, is Mediator off the New Testament betweene GOD and Man, I Tim. 2.5, haveing all power in Heaven and in Earth given vnto him. Mat. 28.18. Being the onely KING, Luke 1.33, being the onely Law-giver, hath in his Testament set downe an absolute, and perfect rule off direction, for

all persons, at all times, to bee observed; Which no Prince, nor anie whosoever, may add to, or diminish from as they will avoid the fearefull judgments denounced against them that shal so do. Revel. 22.18,19. (119)

Smyth died in August 1612. His orphaned congregation still continued to hope for union with the Mennonites. To aid in that process, the members published a confession entitled Propositions and Conclusions . . . 1612–1614. Its one hundred articles are apparently the English version of an earlier Dutch confession drawn up by Smyth. More attention is given to the nature and use of the Bible than in the previous English confessions.

Article 58 of that confession insists "That repentance and faith are wrought in the hearts of men, by the preaching of the word, outwardly in the Scriptures, . . ." (135). Thus the Bible is seen as a convicting and converting word which, nevertheless, can be rejected by the unbeliever. In article 60, Smyth declared the unregenerate need the witness of Scripture.

In articles 61 to 63, however, Smyth argued that "the new creature which is begotten of God needeth not the outward scriptures, creatures or ordinances of the Church, to support or help them. . . ." This article seems to indicate that for Smyth the Bible was not necessary for living the Christian life. However, his meaning becomes clearer in article 63.

> 63. That the new creature although he be above the law and scriptures, yet he can do nothing against the law or scriptures, but rather all his doings shall serve to the confirming and establishing of the law (Rom. iii.31). Therefore he cannot lie, nor steal, nor commit adultery, nor kill, nor hate any man, or do any other fleshly action, and therefore all fleshly libertinism is contrary to regeneration, detestable, and damnable (John viii.34; Rom. vi.15, 17, 18; 2 Pet. ii.18, 19; I John v.18). (135)

The confession itself shows how dependent Smyth's congregation was upon the Bible. It intends to emphasize that the Christian is not of the law but the gospel. In Pauline fashion, Smyth seeks to avoid libertinism (which some may be tempted to embrace in the name of freedom) while affirming that the Christian life is basically a spiritual life nourished by communion with the "Father, the Word, and the Holy Ghost" (135).

A number of General Baptist confessions appeared between 1612 and 1660, the most important in 1660. In the meantime the Baptist movement in England had developed into four distinct groups. In addition to General Baptists, by 1660 there were Particular, Seventh-Day, and Six-Principle Baptists.

After the interregnum (with the abdication of Cromwell's son), as Charles II was preparing to return to England, the Baptists faced a major crisis. They had fared well under Cromwell's regime but they were suspected of treason, since some were implicated in the Fifth Monarchy movement. Therefore, both General and Particular Baptists attempted to set the record straight. The confession which a General Assembly of General Baptists drew up in March 1660 was designed to disavow the false charges of anarchy, armed rebellion, and a conspiracy to murder all who disagreed with them in matters of religion. (All the old charges of alleged crimes of the Anabaptists were revived and used against the Baptists.) The 1660 confession was revised in 1663, and from that date it was known as The Standard Confession. Its preface reads:

A BRIEF CONFESSION OR DECLARATION OF FAITH Set forth by many of us, who are (falsely) called Ana-Baptists, to inform all Men (in these days of scandal and reproach) of our innocent Belief and Practise; for which we are not only resolved to suffer Persecution, to the loss of our Goods, but also Life it self, rather than to decline the same. (224)

Like previous General Baptist confessions, the first articles are concerned with God and a delineation of the redemptive role of Christ. Scripture references are incorporated within the text. A number of articles deal with the Bible.

Article 11 repudiates those "who preach . . . that Scriptureless thing of Sprinkling Infants (*falsely called Baptisme*)," and says that, by such a practice, "the pure *word of God is made of no effect,* and the new Testament-way of bringing in Members, into the Church by regeneration, is cast out." By contrast, the article goes on, what is really "cast out" is "the bond-woman & her son, that is to say, the old Testament-way of bringing in Children into the Church by generation . . ." (228–229).

Article 23 sets forth the General Baptist concept of biblical authority.

> That the holy Scriptures is the rule whereby Saints both in matters of Faith, and conversation (conduct) are to be regulated, they being able to make men wise unto salvation, through Faith in Christ Jesus, profitable for Doctrine, for reproof, for instruction in righteousness, that the man of God may be perfect, throughly furnished unto all good works, 2 Tim. 3.15, 16, 17. John 20.31. Isa. 8.20. (232)

While it is clear that the General Assembly held to the Bible as the rule of faith and practice for their churches, it is also clear that the New Testament alone provided the guidelines for the life of the church. Both testaments testified of Christ who was esteemed the ultimate authority to whom the Scriptures bear witness.

Particular Baptist Confessions

Particular Baptists emerge with separate identifiable congregations in the 1630s. By 1638, a small congregation of Separatists led by John Spilsbury, a cobbler, had begun to advocate believer's baptism. Two or three years later, against the wishes of Spilsbury, the church sent one of its members, a Richard Blunt who understood Dutch, to the Netherlands and the Collegiants, a small Mennonite group at Rhynsburg that practiced immersion. Upon his return to England, immersion was introduced by Blunt who baptized a "Mr. Blacklock." Then together they baptized fifty-one members of, at least, two congregations.

By 1644 there were seven congregations. In that year they published their confession of faith, in part to counteract false charges that had appeared in print. The next year they revised the confession and sent it to Parliament. Parliament was favorably impressed and on March 4, 1647 granted toleration to the Baptists.

This confession is known as The First London Confession, 1644. It antedates The Westminster Confession by two years. While it is Calvinistic, it is only moderately so; that is, it holds to election for salvation but not reprobation. Using as a model A True Confession of 1596, it teaches a fourfold ministry, of "Pastors, Teachers, Elders, Deacons" (166). However, the confession was revised two years later. The Calvinistic pattern of a fourfold ministry was replaced with a twofold ministry of pastors and deacons, a position held by the General Baptists.[6]

The 1644 edition cites numerous Bible references to support the fifty-three articles of the confession. Like A True Confession, these references are not interspersed in the text but reserved as footnotes and placed in the margins, both an innovation and a departure from previous confessions. Two articles, 7 and 8, were devoted to scriptural authority.

VII. The Rule of this Knowledge, Faith, and Obedience, concerning the true worship and service of God, and all other Christian duties, is not mans inventions, opinions, devices, lawes, constitutions, or traditions unwritten whatsoever, but onely the word of God contained in the Canonicall Scriptures. VIII. In this written Word God hath plainly revealed whatsoever he hath thought needfull for us to know, beleeve, and acknowledge, touching the Nature and Office of Christ, in whom all the promises are Yea and Amen to the praise of God. (158)

6. See Article 36 in *The First London Confession 1646 Edition with an Appendix by Benjamin Cox, 1646,* reprint edition (Rochester, New York: Backus Book Publishers, 1981), 10.

Two emphases are worthy of note: reminiscent of the Separatist A True Confession and The General Baptist Confession of 1611, the confession states the Word of God is contained in the canonical Scriptures; and the "written Word" contains all that is necessary regarding Christ. The purpose of Scripture for these Particular Baptists was not to bear witness to itself but to Christ.

The tenth article further underlines the centrality of Christ and the importance of the New Testament:

> Touching his Office, Jesus Christ onely is made the Mediator of the new Covenant, even the everlasting Covenant of grace between God and Man, to be perfectly and fully the Prophet, Priest and King of the Church of God for evermore. (158)

Twelve articles are devoted to Christology. This follows a pattern established in The Waterland Confession and followed in A True Confession. Of the more than three hundred Scripture references, only forty-five are from the Old Testament, and these are never allowed to stand alone without corroborating New Testament references. Therefore, there is an implied principle of interpretation that determines the relationship of the Old and New Testaments on the basis of the finality of the revelation of God in Christ. In the following years The First London Confession went through several subsequent editions, becoming one of the most influential of English Baptist confessions in the seventeenth century.

The Second London Confession 1677–1688

The occasion for The Second London Confession was to demonstrate a substantial measure of agreement with the Presbyterians during a time of renewed persecution. The Clarendon Code, a series of acts passed by Parliament from 1661–1665 to suppress all dissent from the Church of England, was particularly severe on Baptists and Quakers. The Presbyterians, also now numbered among the dissenters, had fared much better, successfully escaping the harshest of

the measures. Therefore, the Baptists and Congregational-
ists felt it would be to their advantage to identify theologically with the Presbyterians. Hence, the Particular Baptists
called for an assembly to consider revising The Westminster
Confession for this purpose.

The Baptists made significant changes in that Presbyterian document to reflect a distinctive Baptist view of the
church, the ordinances, and religious liberty. Before the assembly convened, William Collins, a pastor in London, had
revised it accordingly. Otherwise, The Second London Confession is often word for word identical with the Westminster document.

The 1677 edition contained "An Appendix Concerning
Baptism" and a preface entitled "To the Judicious and Impar-
tial Reader." The preface carries an apology for duplicating
so much of the Westminster Confession.

> . . . we have no itch to clog religion with new words, but to
> readily acquiesce in that form of sound words which hath been,
> in consent with the holy scriptures, used by others before us;
> hereby declaring before God, angels, and men, our hearty agree-
> ment with them, in that wholesome protestant doctrine, which,
> with so clear evidence of scriptures they have asserted. (245)

As in The First London Confession, Scripture references
are placed in the margins. Collins took pains to explain why
he followed this procedure, thus making explicit what had
been implied in Baptist confessions since 1610.

> We have also taken care to affix texts of scripture in the mar-
> gin, for the confirmation of each article in our Confession; in
> which work we have studiously endeavored to select such as are
> most clear and pertinent for the proof of what is asserted by us;
> and our earnest desire is, that all into whose hands this may
> come would follow that (never enough commended) example
> of the noble Bereans, who searched the scriptures daily that
> they might find out whether the things preached to them were
> so or not.

There is one thing more which we sincerely profess, and earnestly desire credence in, viz., that contention is most remote from our design in all that we have done in this matter: and we hope the liberty of an ingenuous unfolding our principles and opening our hearts unto our brethren, with the scripture-grounds on which our faith and practice leans, will by none of them be either denied to us, or taken ill from us. (246)

The Westminster Confession, following the First and Second Helvetic Confessions (Swiss Reformed confessions authored by Heinrich Bullinger in collaboration with other Swiss pastors and theologians), devoted its first ten articles to the Bible, its nature, authority, and interpretation. The Second London Confession followed this section verbatim with two exceptions: (1) the Baptists introduced the first of the ten articles with the phrase, "The Holy Scripture is the only sufficient, certain, and infallible rule of all saving Knowledge, Faith, and Obedience; . . ." (248); and (2) the Baptists rewrote the last phrase of the tenth article. It reads as follows, with the Baptist addition in italics, and the Westminster wording in parentheses:

10. The supream judge by which all controversies of Religion are to be determined, and all Decrees of Councels, opinions of ancient Writers, Doctrines of men, and private Spirits, are to be examined, and in whose sentence we are to rest, can be no other but (the Holy Spirit speaking in Scripture) *the Holy Scripture delivered by the Spirit, into which Scripture so delivered, our faith is finally resolved.* (252)[7]

The Second London Confession marks a departure from previous Baptist confessions. For the first time, articles on the Bible take precedence over articles on God. It is also the first time in any Baptist confession that the Bible is declared "infallible"; or, more precisely, the Bible is declared to be

7. See John H. Leith, *Creeds of the Churches* (Atlanta: John Knox Press, 1982), 196.

"the only . . . infallible rule of all saving Knowledge, Faith, and Obedience."

This exalted view of Scripture is further enhanced in article 5, taken verbatim from the Westminster standard. Article 5 notes that by its perfections the Bible "doth abundantly evidence it self to be the Word of God"; though the article adds that "our full perswasion and assurance of the infallible truth, and divine authority thereof, is from the inward work of the Holy Spirit, bearing witness by and with the Word in our Hearts" (250).

Another edition of The Second London Confession was published in 1688 and was then approved by the Assembly of Particular Baptists with a new preface in 1689. Several other editions followed. One revision, as William Lumpkin notes, "found its way to America . . . and became the body of The Philadelphia Confession, the dominant early Calvinistic Baptist Confession in the New World" (240).

Baptist Confessions in America

As Robert A. Baker has said, "When English Baptists dipped snuff, Baptists in America sneezed." This is to say there was a close relationship between English Baptists and Baptists in the American colonies. All four varieties of English Baptists soon took root in the soil of the New World. However, perhaps due to a mixture of General and Particular Baptists in many congregations, confessions of faith were not immediately forthcoming.

Dr. John Clarke, pastor at Newport, while in jail at Boston in 1651, wrote out his testimony which can be considered a brief and incomplete confession of faith. In this statement of faith there is a veiled reference to the New Testament in article 3 which reads: ". . . and all this according to the last Will and Testament of the living Lord, whose Will is not to be added to or taken from."[8] Here, true to English Baptist

8. H. Shelton Smith, Robert T. Handy, and Lefferts A. Loetscher, *American Christianity: An Historical Interpretation with Representative Documents*, Vol. I (New York: Charles Scribner's Sons, 1960), 168.

confessions before 1677, the emphasis is upon Christ and both the adequacy and reliability of the New Testament account.

The first church confession in the colonies was authored by a Congregationalist turned Baptist, Thomas Goold, pastor of a small Baptist church formed in 1665 at Charlestown, Massachusetts. When the members of the congregation persisted in their separation from the established Congregational Church, they were hauled to jail. In order that the court might have an accurate account of the Baptist faith, the imprisoned presented their confession.

The result, sprinkled with Scripture references, is perhaps the briefest such confession on record, and yet rather well-balanced and complete. Reminiscent of older English Baptist confessions, it began with articles devoted to God, "(a) one god (b) Creator & governor of all things (c) distinguished into father, son, & holy spirit (d) & that this is life eternall to know the only true god & Jesus Christ whom hee hath sent." In reference to the authority of Scripture, the confession reads: "(e) & that the rule of this knowlidge faith & obedience Concerning the worship & service of god & all other Christian duties is the written word of god Contained in the books of the old & new testaments."[9] The phrase, "the written word of God Contained in the books of the old & new testaments," reflects the early English Baptist understanding of the Bible and its authority.

The Philadelphia Confession

Although some churches in the colonies had adopted The Philadelphia Confession by 1712, the Philadelphia Association did not do so until 1742. A few years later the association appointed two pastors, John Gano and Morgan Edwards, for short-term missionary service. They promoted the confession through the South, reorganizing numerous

9. Ibid., 171.

General Baptist churches into Regular (Calvinistic) Baptist churches in the process. However, some General Baptists resisted their efforts.

Separate Baptists, who arose out of the Congregational churches during the First Great Awakening (about 1726–66), were reluctant to issue a confession of faith or subscribe to one, especially The Philadelphia Confession. Finally, however, under the influence of the Second Great Awakening (1795–1830) the Separates and Regulars in Kentucky agreed to unite upon the basis of a confession drawn up for the purpose which became known as The Terms of General Union. Perhaps the key to its acceptance by the Separate Baptists was the ninth article which declared: "And that the preaching Christ tasted death for every man shall be no bar to communion" (359). This article expressed a willingness to accommodate those who still held to a general atonement. The confession asserted the depravity of the sinner as well as the perseverance of the saints.

The first article followed the pattern of The Philadelphia Confession and affirmed "That the Scriptures of the Old and New Testament are the infallible word of God, and the only rule of faith and practice" (359). This reflects the influence of a family of confessions arising out of the Reformed Church of Switzerland.

The Separate Baptists of the Sandy Creek Association in 1816 adopted a confessional statement, Principles of Faith, which reflected the Baptist confessions prior to The Second London Confession when it set forth, in its first article: "We believe that there is only one true and living God; the Father, Son, and Holy Ghost, equal in essence, power, and glory; yet there are not three Gods but one God." Article 2 followed with a statement on the Scriptures, identifying the Old and New Testaments as "the word of God," and its authority as the "only rule of faith and practice" (358).

The New Hampshire Confession

General dissatisfaction with The Philadelphia Confession led the New Hampshire Convention to consider the formulation of a new confession that would considerably modify the Calvinism espoused by The Philadelphia Confession. A confession was approved by the Board of the Convention on January 15, 1833. It received widespread attention when J. Newton Brown, editorial secretary of the American Baptist Publication Society, published it in *The Baptist Church Manual*. J. M. Pendleton included the confession in his church manual. A number of other publications, including the *Bulletin* of Southwestern Baptist Theological Seminary, gave the confession in either its original or one of its revised forms an enhanced status.

The edition published in 1853 contained eighteen articles, the first of which was an exposition of the Scriptures which reads:

> We believe the Holy Bible was written by men divinely inspired, and is a perfect treasure of heavenly instruction; that it has God for its author, salvation for its end, and truth, without any mixture of error, for its matter; that it reveals the principles by which God will judge us; and therefore is, and shall remain to the end of the world, the true centre of Christian union, and the supreme standard by which all human conduct, creeds, and opinions should be tried (361–362).

Although cast in a poetic mold, this high view of the Bible is hardly less exalted than that of The Philadelphia Confession. The phrases "a perfect treasure of heavenly instruction," and "truth, without any mixture of error, for its matter," were apparently phrases in common usage and were probably understood at the time as referring to the Bible's message regarding man and his salvation.

When the Southern Baptist Convention adopted a revised version of The New Hampshire Confession with the addition of ten new articles in 1925, the committee chaired by E. Y. Mullins inserted in the first article "religious" to modify "opinions." This was an extremely significant modification. The remainder of the original article was left unchanged. The committee apparently thought the extensive preface would provide a sufficient guide for understanding and interpreting the entire confession, including its first article.

In 1963, the Convention reproduced the same preface from the 1925 Convention's revision. In addition, the committee added its own statement regarding the nature of Baptist confessions, and then proceeded to revise once again The New Hampshire Confession. The 1963 revision is much longer, more balanced and more complete than the 1925 edition.

The first article on the Scriptures contains significant additions. After the word "inspired" the committee added, "and is the record of God's revelation of Himself to man." A closing sentence is also added, providing an interpretative key: "The criterion by which the Bible is to be interpreted is Jesus Christ."[10] These two additions place this confession closer to the earlier English Baptist confessions than either the first published edition of the New Hampshire or the Philadelphia confessions.

Thus Southern Baptists emerged in the 1960s reaffirming their confidence in the Bible and its authority, while at the same time introducing two significant phrases that attempted to clarify its nature and provide a key for its interpretation.

Conclusion

Admittedly this survey is both limited and selective. Space does not permit a consideration of Primitive or Freewill Baptist confessions. Confessions outside the English and American Baptist experience could not be included. Other local church and associational statements of faith, although important, were not consulted. However, confessions surveyed here can

10. *Annual of the SBC, 1963,* 270.

be considered the most representative and influential within the English and American Baptist historical development.

The earliest confessions were incomplete since they were intent upon emphasizing the distinctive features of the emerging Baptist movement. Too, they indicate kinship with and dependence upon The Waterland Confession (1580), the pioneer confession of the Dutch Mennonites. Although the first two confessions of Smyth lack Scripture references and no one article is given to an exposition of biblical authority, it is assumed that the Bible and particularly the New Testament was the basis for the faith spelled out in the confession. The 1611 Helwys confession includes Scripture references within the text and devotes Article 23 to the Bible. The Smyth congregation's confession of 1612 has an extended discussion of the role of Scripture in the Christian life.

It is significant that in these confessions, as well as The First London Confession (1644) and The Standard Confession (1660), the doctrine of God and an exposition of his trinitarian nature take precedence over an article on the nature and use of the Bible.

With The Second London Confession of 1677 there came a shift in the arrangement of articles. This was the pattern of The Westminster Confession, which followed a family of confessions from the Reformed Church in Switzerland, the First and Second Helvetic Confessions. Therefore, in The Second London Confession and in its revision, The Philadelphia Confession, priority is given to the Bible. It is declared "infallible" and "the Word of God." These confessions say the Old and New Testaments, "being immediately inspired by God, and by his singular care and Providence kept pure in all Ages, are therefore authentical; so as in all controversies of Religion, the Church is finally to appeal unto them" (251).

From this point the best-known Baptist confessions in America followed the order thus established by The Second London Confession. Doubtless the poetic quality of The New Hampshire Confession's article on the Bible as well as the high view of Scripture it espouses endeared it to Southern Baptists. The 1925 and 1963 revisions add interpretative keys in an attempt to compensate for its perceived inadequacy.

It appears then that the Baptist departure from the early seventeenth-century format of their confessions took place with the adaptation of The Westminster Confession in The Second London Confession of 1677. This confession set a pattern which the major Baptist confessions in England and America have followed ever since.

Three notable exceptions were the Charlestown Confession of 1665, the Kehukee Association's confession of 1777, and that of the Sandy Creek Association in 1816. Each of these begins with an article on God and his nature. The articles in each confession devoted to the Bible affirm its authority and its sufficiency in religious matters; none declares the Scriptures inerrant.

The so-called "inerrancy controversy," which first arose outside Southern Baptist life, is now felt within the denomination. This presents a problem. It is difficult to see how Southern Baptists can be more explicit in acknowledging biblical authority than their earliest confessions indicate without becoming guilty of bibliolatry.

When Baptists followed The Westminster Confession in replacing the articles devoted to God with those on the Bible, they unwittingly took a step in this direction. Southern Baptist revisions of The New Hampshire Confession's article on the Bible in 1925 and 1963 reduced the likelihood of this development by emphasizing the religious nature of biblical authority.

We should take heed. The Bible was never intended to take the place of God. Authenticity is essential to the credibility of the biblical witness, of course; and Baptists are among those who have historically viewed the Bible as trustworthy and the only authority in matters of faith and practice. But the Bible's authority is derivative, not ultimate. It is derived from the God who revealed himself finally and completely in Jesus Christ, to whom the Scriptures bear an authentic witness.

12

Is Inerrancy the Issue?
The Lessons of Ridgecrest 1987

ROBISON B. JAMES

One thing was clear to the one thousand participants at the 1987 Ridgecrest Conference on Biblical Inerrancy. Something was *going on,* something momentous not only for Southern Baptists, but also for the entire Christian community. The thing that was not clear was, "*What* is going on in this conference?" The motto might have been, "If you aren't bewildered, you haven't been paying attention." Conferees were expected to listen to thirty-five demanding papers in less than three days.

Moderates "Under the Inerrancy Umbrella"?
Three Approaches

The more I relive the conference by reading the papers and listening to the tapes, however, the less bewildering it is. A bit simplified, the plot of the Ridgecrest drama is that three distinct groups were pulling, pushing, or standing fairly still on this question: *Do such evangelicals as moderate and moderate-conservative Southern Baptists belong "under the inerrancy umbrella" or not?*

1. The first group involved those who gave the featured addresses at Ridgecrest, six of the most eminent inerrantist scholars in the world, all of them non-Southern Baptists. Five of them clearly thought of inerrancy as a rather "large umbrella." They were pulling people under it, so to speak. Two of them were directly saying, and the other three were saying in effect: "Most Southern Baptist moderates, and probably all

177

Southern Baptist moderate-conservatives, belong 'under the umbrella.'"

2. The second group was made up of leading Southern Baptist fundamental-conservatives.[1] Inerrancy in their minds was a "small umbrella." Thus they were forced to push even a great many conservatives out from under it. Indeed, they did more than that. Although they no doubt sincerely believed they were in agreement with the visiting experts, they were in fact pushing at least *half of them* out from under their umbrella, as we shall see.

3. Southern Baptist moderate-conservatives comprised the third group. They "stood fairly still" at Ridgecrest on the umbrella question. It was hard for them to relate to an indistinct "something" (inerrancy) which was at least two different things (242).[2] And further, their dealings had been—and might continue to be—with a rather politicized inerrancy of the "small umbrella" kind.

Concerning "big umbrella" inerrancy, several moderate-conservatives presented carefully reasoned reservations,[3] or posed friendly questions.[4] Generally they avoided and apparently resisted being labeled inerrantists.[5] Some acknowledged that they fit the big-umbrella *definition*, however.[6] Clearly they were not convinced, as a group, that "inerrancy

---

1. As noted and documented in the Preface, this term is used for Southern Baptists who sympathize with the Pressler-Patterson plan to redirect denominational agencies by securing majorities of strict inerrantists on their governing boards. "Moderate-conservatives" sympathize with the opposition to that plan.

2. Here and throughout the rest of this chapter, parenthesized numbers refer to Michael A. Smith, ed., *Proceedings of the Conference on Biblical Inerrancy 1987* (Nashville: Broadman, 1987). The immediate reference above is to remarks made by Frank Pollard.

3. For example, John Lewis (129–134), and William Hull (62–64, 81–84).

4. Especially Peter Rhea Jones (190–197).

5. Peter Rhea Jones prefers "infallible" (216–218).

6. For example, Frank Pollard (242), and very guardedly, James Flamming (142).

language" would strengthen Southern Baptists' historically high view of Scripture.[7]

Clark Pinnock: "Chicago Includes You Both"

Visiting inerrantist historian Mark Noll explicitly pulled Southern Baptist moderates under the inerrancy umbrella by describing the "Baptist way" of upholding a fully truthful Bible (9–19). This uncomplicated, pietist approach is equivalent to the "simple biblicism" explained in the Introduction to this book. And, more to the point, this approach is also the prevailing attitude toward the Bible among Southern Baptist moderates.

Another of the visiting inerrantists went beyond Noll, however, in pulling moderates under the umbrella of inerrancy. "Appearances can be deceiving," said Canadian theologian Clark Pinnock.

> It looks as if you have a fight over biblical inerrancy in the Convention, but you do not. What you have is a fight over how inerrancy is to be defined: whether in an elaborate tight manner or in a more open, permissive way. The irony of it is that the Chicago Statement, which the militants [aggressive strict inerrantists] say they endorse, encompasses both your positions. Like the militants it speaks of complete errorlessness but like the moderates it also speaks of the lack of technical precision and the topical arrangement of material and such like (77, and see 98).

That is, the 1978 Chicago Statement of the ICBI (International Council on Biblical Inerrancy) acknowledges that the following things are found in the Bible, but says they should not be viewed as errors: events recounted out of chronological order, numbers disagreeing, divergent accounts of the same events, words attributed to other parts of the Bible which are only loose quotations, etc. These and several other types of apparent error are listed, and declared not to be errors, in the famous "Article 13" of the ICBI statement.

7. James E. Carter was forthright (25–31).

The Chicago Statement, Pinnock urged, was designed to hold together within evangelicalism the same groups, "militants and moderates," which are divided by such acrimony within the Southern Baptist Convention. The Statement speaks wholesomely "with a forked tongue," he explained (77). It "papers over this disagreement by compromise wording as virtually all creeds do. There is lots of rhetoric to satisfy the fundamentalists, and then there is Article 13 for the liberal inerrantists to flee to" (97).[8]

Thus, Pinnock observed, inerrancy is not a "firm and clear category." Though it is supposed to answer our problems, "the inerrantists themselves cannot agree on what it signifies." And the reason is that "the biblical writers did not compose their work with the elaborate theory of inerrancy to guide them." Thus they wrote "hundreds of things which are hard for us who do have [the theory] to reconcile with it." And that is bound to happen, he stated, whenever a person tries "to impose on the Scriptures a human theory not itself scriptural. . . . It just does not work. The text will resist it" (97, 98).

Pinnock continued, "even though honest inerrantists surely must know that their favorite category is not clear or firm, some of them are intent upon ramming the strict version of it down the throats of others." He then issued an appeal: "since according to the Chicago Statement biblical inerrancy is an open and flexible category, closely resembling the simpler biblicism of the moderates, what are you fighting over? Why not just declare peace? Chicago declares almost all of us inerrantists" (98).

Inerrantists' Surprising Concessions

Besides Noll and Pinnock, three of the other four visiting inerrantists at Ridgecrest qualified what they meant by

8. Thus understood, the Chicago Statement has the kind of "affirmative ambiguity" which a Baptist confession must have, according to the Baptist Faith and Message. See the editor's introduction to chapter 10, p. 141.

"inerrancy" so extensively that Southern Baptist moderates would fit under their "large inerrancy umbrella."[9]

The Chicago Statement's list of qualifications in Article 13 is extensive. But it probably would not prepare the reader for such qualifications as the following:

"In most cases," said Kenneth Kantzer, "the words of Jesus cited in the Gospels are not to be thought of as direct quotes. They usually give us not the exact equivalent of his Greek or Aramaic words but the sense of what he said. This is often true even when the words are in the form of direct quotation" (116). Similarly, Kantzer acknowledged that there are discrepancies between Stephen's speech in Acts 7 and the accounts in Genesis. The inerrancy of Scripture may only mean that what Stephen said, including his minor mistakes, was inerrantly recorded (116).

Millard Erickson believes it is consistent with inerrancy to conclude that Matthew gathered into chapters 5–7 "sayings given by Jesus on more than one occasion," and that it was not all spoken by Jesus in the Sermon on the Mount (178).

J. I. Packer points out that "all the historians of the ancient world reported what people said by a convention that is the exact opposite of ours. If they knew the substance of what was said, they felt free to construct a speech, sentences and paragraphs of direct speech, in which words were put into the mouth of the character." The biblical writers used that convention (210, 211).

And though he believes Genesis 2 and 3 teach that there was a first man and woman, Adam and Eve, Packer comments: "What is less certain is whether all the physical details of the narrative are meant to inform us what we would in fact have

---

9. Dr. Robert D. Preus accepted enough qualifications that somewhat the same could be said of him, too (51–55). But he alone of the six visiting scholars said the historical-critical method is so governed by naturalistic presuppositions that rejecting it is a logical concomitant of believing in Scripture (56–60). "I would say that Dr. Preus made an error there, and I would attack him on that point," said Kantzer in a May 6 news conference at Ridgecrest. Audiotape in the editor's possession.

seen happen had we been there, or whether God means them
to function as significant symbols only" (212). In his prepared
text he gave examples of the kind of symbolism he had in
mind: "snake = Satan, fruit = an alluring option, garden = a
state of unalloyed pleasure, etc."[10]

Lordship, Not Scholarship—The Small Umbrella

Leading Southern Baptist fundamental-conservatives make
two conciliatory moves. First, as Convention President Adrian
Rogers said, they do not insist upon the word "inerrancy"
(128). And second, they make a distinction between the *interpretation* and the *identity* of the Bible. Richard Land of
Criswell College touched off a chorus of Amens from much
of the audience at Ridgecrest when he said, with enormous
emphasis, that the issue in dispute is not how one interprets
the Bible but what the Bible *is*.[11]

The fundamental-conservatives are certainly sincere, and
their second move in particular could be very promising. But
the very distinction they see as important is not always observed in what they say. One of their most emphasized points
about Jesus' Lordship appears to be based on a failure to
distinguish between what the Bible is, and how we interpret
parts of it.

This was illustrated in a striking way at Ridgecrest by H.
Edwin Young. The pastor of Houston's Second Baptist
Church said he understood "inerrancy" in the sense that
"Adam and Eve were historical figures. There really was an
ark and a great flood. Two million plus Israelites were fed
with manna in the wilderness and Jonah was swallowed by a
great fish." Since in Young's view Jesus believed those things,
inerrancy in that sense "is not a question of scholarship. It is,
it always has been, and it always will be a question of Lordship" (171, 172).

This means that anyone who does not accept certain speci-

---

10. J. I. Packer, "Problem Areas Related to Biblical Inerrancy" (5).
11. The editor's personal notes of May 4, 1987. Compare also Gene
Williams (251, 252).

fied interpretations of portions of Scripture has rejected Christ's Lordship. Even to ask in a scholarly way whether these interpretations of biblical passages are correct is spurning the Lord who died for us. In the sentence before he took that stand, Young said, "Inerrancy is not a dividing point. It is a rallying point." But it is hard to imagine a more divisive stand than saying someone who differs with my interpretation rejects Jesus Christ as Lord.

In a discussion after his talk, Young reluctantly conceded to a reporter that he had adopted one interpretation of what Jesus and the Bible mean to teach about Adam, Eve, the flood, the Israelites in the wilderness, Jonah, and inerrancy, and that there are other responsible interpretations of Jesus besides his. (He knew about "Jesus' View of Scripture," an article which now appears as chapter 2 in this book.) "But," he added, "these other interpretations don't belong in this conference."[12]

In the afternoon following Young's address, at a news conference with all three of the ranking inerrantists present, these speakers disagreed with him roundly. Kenneth Kantzer stated that people who are not inerrantists do not necessarily reject the Lordship of Christ. "One of the finest examples," he added, "is a person who stands very, very high in my book, C. S. Lewis."[13]

Packer noted that some inerrantists believe Jesus was referring to Jonah somewhat as we might refer to Hamlet. He himself believes that view is not the more probable. But in any case, he stated, as with all matters of exegesis or interpretation, it is a question of what will pass muster within the arena of scholarly discussion, and whether the probabilities are strong enough that we may be certain. We might paraphrase Packer: It is a question of scholarship, not Lordship.

At this juncture, Pinnock interjected that what Packer had just said "makes him a 'liberal' according to Southern Baptist 'militants.' Let's be honest about this. Believing that is not

12. The editor's personal notes of May 6, 1987.
13. Audiotape in the editor's possession.

open to them." In other words, Packer is *not an inerrantist* in the sense leading Southern Baptist fundamental-conservatives have in mind (even though he is a charter member of the ICBI and one of the main drafters of its key statements).[14]

The same is true of Millard Erickson,[15] and probably of Kantzer as well. Thus, counting Pinnock, at least half the eminent inerrantist scholars at Ridgecrest would not be acceptable under the small Southern Baptist umbrella.

Asked in the news conference whether he was an inerrantist, Pinnock answered, "I am and I'm not, because the thing is so ambiguous." Motioning to Kantzer and Packer he said, "In the sense in which they are, I am. But," he added, bringing down the house, "are *they* inerrantists?"

Is inerrancy the issue among moderate and conservative Protestants—inerrancy as distinguished from certain interpretations of specific biblical texts?

Not if the Southern Baptist controversy is an indication. As was so often the case at Ridgecrest, it was Pinnock who stated matters without equivocation: " . . . the real challenge here . . . ," he said, "is an attempt to impose upon the Southern Baptist Convention a whole set of beliefs by force and not really a debate over inerrancy at all" (100).

---

14. Packer's position is subtle: Various things may be said, various statements made, by the paragraphs and sentences in Scripture. But do they fall within the scope of what the authors (including God) *intended to express*? If not, even if some are false, there is no error. Where no assertion is intended, no error can be committed (see 138, 205–207). "Error is an affirmation, an assertion, which fails to be veridical when it seeks to be veridical" (205).

A Packer-type inerrantist is free to say every physical detail in the Adam and Eve story is factually false (in the video-recording sense) if that person goes on sincerely to say that these physical details are *not what the authors intend to say.* On the basis of other biblical testimony Packer is confident that part of the intended assertion in the story is that there was an original pair, our forebears, who sinningly initiated humankind's fallen condition. (Compare Romans 5, for example.)

15. See pp. 178–180, and Millard J. Erickson, *Christian Theology,* vol. 1 (Grand Rapids: Baker, 1983), 233–238.

Afterword

CLARK H. PINNOCK

It seems a crying shame to me that a world-class evangelical (and successfully evangelistic) denomination like the Southern Baptist Convention—the great preponderance of whose members by all accounts hold fast to the everlasting gospel of Jesus Christ according to the Scriptures—should be embroiled in a bitter and painful struggle ostensibly over the theory of biblical inerrancy and how tightly it should be drawn and defined. Christians have never agreed on the details of this belief, yet that has never before prevented them working together in the defense and proclamation of the gospel. Why should it now?

The tragedy is compounded by the fact that it is also so unnecessary. For if we take the Chicago statement as the definition of what inerrancy signifies (and what other definition is there of such authority and stature?), we find the large majority of Southern Baptists able to find room under its generous provisions. Its version of inerrancy which permits us to recognize the apparent exceptions listed in its Article 13 scarcely poses much of a problem to the essentially conservative Southern Baptist moderates. (There may be a few exceptions to this, but not many, I would judge.) It causes me to wonder—has the Enemy cooked up this fight among God's people to try and prevent them posing the threat to his dark kingdom which this great denomination does, in fact, represent when it is united?

Nevertheless, to get some perspective, we need to realize that the roots of this controversy go a long way back into the history of Christianity. The notion that the Bible was verbally dictated by God so that it owed virtually nothing to the actual human writers and everything to God himself was a view held by some of the earliest Christian (not to mention, Jewish) theologians. In the second century, Athenagoras saw the prophets as flutes played upon by the divine flute player, while Gregory the Great believed the human writers were no more than pens held in the hand of the divine Author.

Mechanical views which drastically minimize the human role in the composition of the Scriptures have been around for a very long time. They stem from the (I think) commendable desire to defend the Word of God from any criticism, real or imagined. In the name of defending the Bible, conservatives have often resorted in the past to elaborate theories about the biblical text which have the effect of denying that the Bible is in any real sense a truly human as well as divine word. I think if we would just recognize how long this debate has been with us (it certainly did not begin with the present struggle), we might find it possible to exercise greater patience and extend more understanding to those who are similarly burdened in this way. Over-belief in regard to the Bible has been a problem for centuries, and getting upset and angry about it is not going to do any good.

The answer has to be old-fashioned love and understanding. We must appreciate and love those who see the necessity of defending the Bible, even in what may seem excessive ways, and welcome them graciously in our common Lord. And further, we must continue the work of educating people, as this book does so well, in a more intelligent and mature understanding of what the Bible really is and how it actually functions as an authority in the churches. The writers of the Bible were not mere copyists or secretaries, but flesh-and-blood people like ourselves, giving us the fruit of their efforts to hear God speak to them in the context of their special places in history. In seeking to correct an unbalanced over-belief which overlooks the human and historical dimension of the Bible, let us never fail to express our unsurpassed confidence in the divine treasure which the Bible surely is. Let us not fight over it, but try to study and proclaim it together, as we take the gospel of the kingdom to the nations.

I think we are on the road to a sound and sensible doctrine of Scripture, however battle-weary some may feel just now. In the church at large, the liberal theologians forsook the Bible, and now quite properly the people are forsaking them. Conservatives have won the day, and are now trying to get the wrinkles out of their sounder view of inspiration. It is natural, pendulum-like that over-belief should replace under-belief in the doctrine of Scripture for a season. But in time I believe we will see sense and balance restored—sooner rather than later would be my hope.

Selected Bibliography

In this book, complete bibliographical information is supplied for every source cited within a chapter at the point where the title is first cited. To facilitate further reading, sixteen of the titles cited earlier are included here, and another twenty-one are added.

The Southern Baptist Situation

The second of Professor Garrett's titles below is an extremely valuable bibliographical essay. After he treats E. Y. Mullins and W. T. Conner in depth, Garrett gives perceptive thumbnail sketches of more than eighty writings by "Southern Baptist author-theologians since 1952," twenty-six writings on inerrancy alone. Many of these writings appeared in three independent Southern Baptist publications: the fundamentalist *Southern Baptist Journal* (started 1973), the fundamental-conservative *Southern Baptist Advocate* (started 1980), and the moderate-conservative *SBC Today* (started 1983).

The second and fourth entries below are inerrantist, while the other Southern Baptist entries are noninerrantist, qualifiedly inerrantist, or written by authors of differing views.

Allen, Clifton J. "The Book of the Christian Faith." In *The Broadman Bible Commentary* vol. 1. Nashville: Broadman, 1969, 1–14.

Bush, L. Russ, and Nettles, Tom J. *Baptists and the Bible.* Chicago: Moody, 1980.

Dilday, Russell H., Jr. *The Doctrine of Biblical Authority.* Nashville: Convention Press, 1982.

Draper, James T., Jr. *Authority: The Critical Issue for Southern Baptists.* Old Tappan, N.J.: Revell, 1984.

Garrett, James Leo. "Biblical Authority According to Baptist Confessions of Faith." *Review and Expositor* 76 (Winter 1979), 43–54.

_____. "The Teaching of Recent Southern Baptist Theologians on the Bible." In Michael A. Smith, ed., *Proceedings of the*

Conference on Biblical Inerrancy 1987. Nashville: Broadman, 1987, 289–315; bibliography on pp. 546–53.

Honeycutt, Roy L. "Biblical Authority: A Treasured Heritage!" *Review and Expositor* 83 (Fall 1986), 605–22. Republished as a pamphlet, slightly revised, by Southern Baptist Theological Seminary, Louisville, Kentucky, 1987.

Hull, William E. "Shall We Call the Bible Infallible?" *Crescent Hill Sermons*. Louisville, Ky.: Crescent Hill Baptist Church, 1970.

Humphreys, Fisher, ed. *The Controversy in the Southern Baptist Convention*. New Orleans: Faculty of the New Orleans Baptist Theological Seminary, 1985.

James, Gordon H. *Inerrancy and the Southern Baptist Convention*. Dallas: Southern Baptist Heritage Press, 1986.

James, Robison B. "Biblical Authority or Inerrancy?" *SBC Today* 3 (November, 1985), 1, 6, 7.

_____. "Baptist Faith and Message Statement: Best Answer." *SBC Today* 4 (October 1986), 8, 9.

Smith, Michael A. *Proceedings of the Conference on Biblical Inerrancy 1987*. Nashville: Broadman, 1987.

Summers, Ray. "Contemporary Approaches in New Testament Study." In *The Broadman Bible Commentary* vol. 8, Nashville: Broadman, 1969, 48–58.

Noninerrantist or Qualifiedly Inerrantist Sources

Achtemeier, Paul J. *The Inspiration of Scripture: Problems and Proposals*. Philadelphia: Westminster, 1980.

Barr, James. *Beyond Fundamentalism*. Philadelphia: Westminster, 1984.

Boer, Harry R. *The Bible and Higher Criticism*. Grand Rapids: Eerdmans, 1981.

Davis, Stephen T. *The Debate about the Bible: Inerrancy versus Infallibility*. Philadelphia: Westminster, 1977.

Dunn, James D. G. "The Authority of Scripture According to Scripture." *Churchman* 96 (1982), 104–22, 201–25.

Erickson, Millard J. *Christian Theology* vol. 1. Grand Rapids: Baker, 1983.

Hayes, John H., and Holladay, Carl R. *Biblical Exegesis: A Beginner's Handbook*. Atlanta: John Knox, 1982.

James, Robison B. "The Quarrel Between Inerrancy and Sola Scriptura." *Journal of Faith and Thought* 4 (Spring 1986), 2–13.

McKim, Donald K., ed. *The Authoritative Word: Essays on the Nature of Scripture.* Grand Rapids: Eerdmans, 1983.

Pinnock, Clark H. *The Scripture Principle.* San Francisco: Harper & Row, 1984.

Price, Robert M. "Inerrant the Wind: The Troubled House of North American Evangelicals." *Evangelical Quarterly* 55 (July 1983), 129–44.

Rogers, Jack B., and McKim, Donald K. *The Authority and Interpretation of the Bible: An Historical Approach.* San Francisco: Harper & Row, 1979.

Rogers, Jack B., ed. *Biblical Authority.* Waco, Tex.: Word, 1977.

Inerrantist Sources

Archer, Gleason L. *Encyclopedia of Bible Difficulties.* Grand Rapids: Zondervan, 1982.

Carson, D. A., and Woodbridge, John D., eds. *Scripture and Truth.* Grand Rapids: Zondervan, 1983.

Geisler, Norman L., ed. *Inerrancy.* Grand Rapids: Zondervan, 1979.

Hodge, A. A., and Warfield, B. B. *Inspiration.* Roger R. Nicole, ed. Grand Rapids: Baker, 1979.

Lindsell, Harold L. *The Battle for the Bible.* Grand Rapids: Zondervan, 1976.

Montgomery, John W., ed. *God's Inerrant Word.* Minneapolis: Bethany Fellowship, 1974.

Nicole, Roger, and Michaels, J. Ramsey, eds. *Inerrancy and Common Sense.* Grand Rapids: Baker, 1980.

Noll, Mark A., ed. *The Princeton Theology 1812–1921.* Phillipsburg, N.J.: Presbyterian and Reformed, 1983.

Radmacher, Earl D., and Preus, Robert D., eds. *Hermeneutics, Inerrancy and the Bible.* Grand Rapids: Zondervan, 1984.

Woodbridge, John D. *Biblical Authority: A Critique of the Rogers/McKim Proposal.* Grand Rapids: Zondervan, 1982.